ISBN 978-0-282-94784-2
PIBN 10866599

1 MONTH OF
FREE
READING

at

www.ForgottenBooks.com

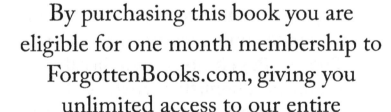

By purchasing this book you are eligible for one month membership to ForgottenBooks.com, giving you unlimited access to our entire collection of over 1,000,000 titles via our web site and mobile apps.

To claim your free month visit: www.forgottenbooks.com/free866599

TURKEY AND THE WAR BY

VLADIMIR JABOTINSKY

(War Correspondent of the " Russkia Vedomosti " of Moscow).

LONDON

T. FISHER UNWIN, LTD

ADELPHI TERRACE

First published in 1917

It is my pleasant duty gratefully to acknowledge that—so far as the linguistic form of this essay is concerned—the following pages were written with the friendly and constant collaboration of Miss Violet Ross-Johnson.

V. J.

CONTENTS

PART I : THE AIM OF THIS WAR

PART II : THE INNER STATE OF TURKEY

vii

CONTENTS

PART I—THE AIM OF THIS WAR

I—AIMS AND CAUSES

14—AIMS AND CAUSES

AIMS AND CAUSES

THIS little book is an attempt to define the real aims of the present war. That is to say, we presume that there may be a difference between what people, even people in leading positions, suppose to be the aim of the war, and what it really is. The current formulas on this subject circulated in this country may prove, on more attentive analysis, to reflect popular feelings rather than immanent realities of the universal situation. Mr. Asquith's well-known statement, twice repeated in 1914 and 1916, is perhaps one instance. Noble in spirit and energetic in form though it be, it cannot pretend to give a full enumeration of all the problems involved in the actual conflict. Even more : some points upon which it dwelt are, perhaps, not so important as other points which it did not mention.

To be sure, popular feeling plays a great rôle in every war. The masses of a belligerent country must have before them a clear goal for which they think it worth while to fight ; and this constitutes, as a German would say, the " subjective " aim of the war. But besides this, perhaps above this, there is the " objective " aim. It is, in some way, independent of the people's mood or inclination. It is inherent in the situation, produced and imposed by the force of things.

AIMS AND CAUSES

What is the way to find out these "objective" aims in the intricacies of the present conflict? First of all, by defining its causes. That is to say, from among the different things which are generally quoted as "causes of the war" we must separate those which made the war inevitable. Analysing the different factors, we shall easily see that many of them would not have been able by themselves to provoke so enormous a conflagration; they may have added fuel, but did not make the fire; whilst a few of them, or perhaps just one of them, would inevitably have produced the conflict even if the others had not existed. The removal of these essential roots of the struggle is the natural immanent aim of the war. Without this, the settlement would not be effective even if the secondary causes were removed, and a new and perhaps more terrible war must follow.

In dealing with this analysis we must ignore every sentimental consideration. Some battlecries which excite our greatest sympathies may prove, on test, to be of secondary importance ; in that case we shall have to accept the truth and to draw from it the necessary solutions, however unpalatable they may be. Again, what our inquiry ascertains to be the " real aim " may not in itself inspire us with enthusiasm : but we must submit to its imperative necessity and carry it through.

To make our meaning still clearer let us have recourse to an old-fashioned but still useful device: to the parable. Imagine an old town in which an epidemic disease suddenly breaks out.   People are naturally anxious to discover the source of the scourge and to remove it. Some think that the cause lies in the absence of vegetation ; others say that the streets of the town are too narrow and the houses too dark. Others again insist on the necessity of improving the underground drainage. Thus a complete scheme of reconstruction of the old town is formed, which attracts sympathies and excites enthusiasms. It works its own way further : Mr. Somebody is suddenly reminded of his own old feud with his neighbour, a field-boundary dispute unjustly decided by the court, and he goes around saying that there can be no health where there is no justice, and that a radical struggle against the disease implies a reform of the tribunals—and the revision of some old quarrels. But the Doctor knows that the real cause of the epidemic is the bad quality of the potable water, because the source from which it comes is infected ; and to disinfect it the picturesque beauty of the river-margin must be deformed by a plain but hygienic embankment. That is the difficulty, because many of his fellow-citizens love the romantic river-side in its wildness. So the Doctor says : " Your scheme is very good. I grant you, green spaces are necessary : wide streets and bright houses are healthy : a more perfect drainage is of the greatest importance. I even agree with the desirability of a reform of the courts. Try it all if you can. I shall be glad if you succeed. But don't forget that even if you succeed in all this you don't destroy the root of our plague, and it will persist. If you want to get rid of it you must embank the river. That is the main thing—that is *the* thing to be done. I know you don't like it; but I can't count with your nice feelings in this question. Drop the whole scheme if necessary, but remember the river."

The popular list of the " aims of the war " includes the freedom of small nationalities, a fair solution of the Alsace problem, and what people call the destruction of Prussian militarism. We intentionally abstain from mentioning such axioms as the restoration of Belgium : it is a holy and imperative duty of the Allies, but the redressing of a consequence of the war cannot be considered as one of those aims

which determine or underlie human conflagrations. Nor will we indulge in such
beautiful ideals as the " prohibition " of
wars and the creation of a compulsory
International Tribunal—we are dealing
with plain realities, not with ideals. On
the other hand, the three points mentioned
just above are certainly within the bounds
of practical politics. Everybody to whom
freedom is not merely an empty word
must fully recognise that their realisation
would be a blessing for humanity ; and
he will encourage the Allies to insist, cost
what might, upon this noble platform.
Its fulfilment, we hope, will be the consequence of the war ; but we are now
concerned with the causes. Let it therefore be said at once, without further pre-
amble, that the present war owes its birth

directly and beyond doubt to the problem of the Near and Middle East.

We strongly reject every suspicion that we are underrating the great value of such principles as protection of the smaller nations, the re-annexation of Alsace-Lorraine, and the taming of the shrew whose name is German Junkerdom. It would indeed be a heavy disappointment, perhaps a moral disaster for the civilised world if these goals could not be attained in connection with this war. But the root of the present plague is in Asia Minor, and the first and last aim of the war is the solution of the Eastern question.

In the following chapters we shall try to recall the facts and arguments which led us to this conclusion.

II—THE ALLEGED AIMS OF THE WAR

II.—THE ALLIED AIMS OF THE WAR.

II

THE ALLEGED AIMS OF THE WAR

(a) *Freedom of Small Nationalities*

Is the establishment of the freedom of small nations an indispensable aim of the war, a *conditio sine qua non* of peace? This question is tantamount to another one: was it the absence of such freedom that caused the war?

Let some serious and unsweetened words be said on this subject. The list of small nationalities to whom freedom is denied is very long. It includes not only the Slavs, Roumanians, Italians of Germany, Austria and Hungary, not only the

Armenians of Turkey. It includes also the Finns, Poles, Ukrainians, Jews and many, many other small peoples—Armenians not excepted—in Russia. Some malignant people may add that it includes so far the Irish nation which has no more autonomy than Poland. And, since we place among the oppressed nations the Czechs, who possess two Universities where their language is predominant, it may be worth while to mention the Flemish of Belgium for whom the "flamandisation" of the Ghent Academy is still only a hope of the future. We do not inquire who was right and who was wrong in all these cases. We do not even intend to repeat, "Physician, heal thyself." But one thing is obvious: the sufferings of the smaller nationalities, taken alone, could not have provoked a European conflict. Our sympathy with them does not go so far—and none of the greater belligerent countries ever seemed disposed to draw the sword for their sake. Italy was the ally of the ruler of the Trentino and Istria; Austria, where the Poles were all-powerful, was the ally of Germany where Polish children were forbidden to pray to God in Polish; and the sincerest sympathy with the descendants of Kosciuszko did not prevent France from concluding the alliance with Russia and from keeping silence over everything that happened in Warsaw. It is useless to insist further upon this point, except to say that the *status quo* of many small nationalities could have yet lasted for years and years without provoking a conflict between Great Powers. The recognition of this truth compels us to conclude that even after this war a quite durable peace could be signed and kept without implying any radical improvement in the condition of subject peoples. This plain truth is so well understood elsewhere that the French insist upon " freedom of small nations " with much less emphasis than the English, and official Russia with still less.

(b) *Alsace-Lorraine*

The Great War has shown that France keeps the memory of Alsace-Lorraine with a freshness almost unaffected by time. For many observers this fact seemed little short of a revelation. André Lichtenberger, in a book on Alsace published in 1912, told us how a French captain had asked fifty recruits : " What is Alsace ? " Thirty-eight of them had answered " à peu près convenablement," whilst twelve—that is a quarter of the whole—" ignoraient de quoi il s'agissait." On the other side, the younger generations in the annexed provinces passed through the German schools, while they were artificially severed from any French influence ; considerable numbers of German " immigrés," especially from Prussia, had been poured into the country, so that Metz, for instance, had in 1907, out of 6,450 electors, 4,300 immigrants and only 2,150 natives. The psychological effects of these circumstances seemed to be undeniable ; and we have only to recall René Bazin's novel " Les Oberlé " in order to remind our readers that indifference towards France and inclination to a lasting settlement with Berlin were not limited exclusively to the new-comers, but showed themselves even amongst the old Alsatian families.

The political elections gave what seemed even a more striking test of this change of spirit. In 1887 all the fifteen deputies which the annexed provinces returned to the Reichstag belonged to the Alsace-Lorraine party ; in 1912 only nine remained faithful to the old banner of provincial particularism—the other six seats were conquered by different Imperial parties. These figures seem to speak very clearly, especially if compared with the numbers of the Polish club in the same Reichstag which, from thirteen in 1887, rose to eighteen in 1912—in spite of a German immigration to Posen far more formidable than that to Alsace. Even after the war began the *Temps*, discussing the probabilities of a referendum in Alsace-Lorraine on the question of re-annexation, seemed to be not completely sure of a unanimous reply.

But the apprehension on both sides proved rather groundless. The Prussians themselves had the happy inspiration, through the famous incident of Zabern which happened just on the eve of the war, to refresh and strengthen all the grievances and bitternesses of the Alsatian heart, and it is now officially admitted in Germany that the attitude of the native population in the Imperial land is " not satisfactory." Alsace has not forgotten France.

Nor has France forgotten Alsace. The

war has at once revived the old love that slept, but was alive; and to-day, if any fifty recruits were asked " What is Alsace ? " every man would reply : " It is what we are fighting for."

This mutual faith after half a century of severation is one of the most impressive features of this war. But in trying to weigh the exact part it plays in the present conflict we must be careful to avoid any exaggeration. Now that France is at war, she wants to recover her own fringes whose children long to return home. But it would be a striking injustice to democratic France, even an outrageous calumny, to say that France would have ever willingly provoked the war, even for that holy cause. None of her enemies, certainly none of her friends could admit such a possibility. The Revanche party had never, in the course of the last decades, arisen to a strength sufficient to influence the foreign policy of the French Republic. If this war had not come France would certainly have continued to keep a Memory and a Will in the depths of her national heart, but her actual policy would still have remained as it was seen to be on the occasion of Agadir—a policy tending to peace and prepared for sacrifices for the sake of peace. The question of Alsace cannot be considered as a cause of the war. We must insist upon this, and insist, first of all, in fairness to France, whose hands bear no stain of all this blood.

We hope our words will be rightly understood. Even supposing that the present war proves unable to solve such questions as Alsace-Lorraine, the Trentino, or Poland, that will not imply that the concerned nations renounce their respective claims. Neither France nor Alsace will ever reconcile themselves with the brutal fact of 1871 ; never will Italy forget the *terre irredente* ; the Polish nation will strive and struggle against her three rulers, just as the other nationalities of Russia and Austria-Hungary will never bow to their yoke. But the nature of all these aspirations does not necessarily imply a European war as the only, or even the main way of realization. Other ways are open—internal developments of the backward countries, international bargains and compensations in the case of eventual oversea acquisitions, and in general that

vague but still undeniable thing which
we call progress. It may assume forms
of revolution or evolution ; in either case
it is a slow process, certainly much slower
than a decision enforced by war. But we
can be assured that everybody in the
civilized countries of Europe will prefer
the slow way to a repetition of the universal horror that is passing before our
eyes. Now that the world is at war, the
Allies must undoubtedly do their utmost
to achieve a fair settlement of the mentioned ethnical and territorial problems ;
but a failure in this regard, sad though it
would be, is not likely to set the world
at war again.

(c) *Militarism*

What is meant by " destruction of
Prussian militarism " ? Mr. Asquith, the

35

responsible author of the phrase, gave an explanation of it some time ago that seemed to restrict its meaning very closely. He said : " As a result of the war we intend to establish the principle that international problems must be handled by free negotiations on equal terms between free peoples, and that this settlement shall no longer be hampered and swayed by the overmastering dictation of a Government controlled by a military caste. That is what I mean by the destruction of the military domination of Prussia."

Put this way the crushing of Prussian militarism is an obvious necessity. It cannot even be said to be one of the distinct aims of the war—it is simply an essential and inherent element of victory. The victory of the Allies, whatever be the peace terms after the struggle is won, will naturally imply the liquidation of the German dream of an " overmastering dictation." Perhaps it can be said that the buzzing of this dream has been already stopped even in the most sanguine German heads. It is already killed, the victory of the Allies will bury it for ever.

But this sensible and obviously fair scheme has nothing to do with the destruction of militarism. Militarism is a system applied nowadays in the majority of civilized countries : it consists in employing a big part of the State's resources, directly or indirectly, for armaments. It is a very wicked system ; it obstructs the development of education and social reforms ; it poisons the soul of the civilized peoples ; the removal of it would be a blessing for the world. But it is clear that it cannot be removed in Prussia without being removed at the same time and in the same measure in all the other countries. It is again the old question of limitation of armaments— a question of ideals, while we must not forget that in this war we are dealing with realities.

It is a favourite formula with many of us to say that militarism by itself is a mutual provocation to war, that the weight of military expenditures in the different countries compels them, as it were, to make good their sacrifices by utilizing the formidable weapons which they have accumulated. It may be true. But there are truths which, like medals, have their reverse. The facts of the last thirty-five years of world's history hardly suggest that militarism means frequency of wars between militaristic countries. It cannot be denied that the last decades which witnessed an unparalleled flourishing of militarism, have been just those in which conflagrations between Great Powers have occurred much more seldom than before. The only real exception was the Russo-Japanese war. The Spanish-American war was a conflict between two nations to which the reproach of militarism can hardly be applied. The same must be said of the Anglo-Boer war : as a land-power England has never been accused of " militarism " even in pacifist pamphlets. The Italian Tripoli campaign was rather a military expedition than a war : it is enough to recall that the Italian casualties in the conquest of

Tripoli amounted to a few thousands. The Chino-Japanese war belonged to the same category, and also the European expedition against the Boxers. In the Græco-Turkish war, and in the two recent Balkan wars, however cruel the latter may have been, none of the leading militaristic Powers were engaged. The leading militaristic Powers managed to avoid the danger for a longer period than would have been possible in the middle of the nineteenth century, when armaments were cheap and childish in comparison with ours of to-day. The long European peace may have been a chance; but it may have been also, and perhaps with more probability, a consequence of the formidable development of armaments. Knowing what it costs in money and guessing what it might cost in human lives, the Great Powers felt naturally afraid of taking irreparable steps. Buckle proved that the invention of gunpowder, instead of increasing the frequency of wars, diminished it in a very considerable proportion. The cheaper the easier—it is a rule for wars as for goods. All this will certainly not prevent us from hating militarism; but on the other hand there is no direct proof that the present war is simply or mainly " a result of excessive armaments." Militarism is responsible for the cruel character of the tragedy, but the causes of the tragedy are to be found in the presence of conflicting interests, not of modern weapons. The liquidation of militarism, in Prussia and everywhere, is a thing fair, holy and necessary, but it is not one of the natural, objective, immanent aims of the Great War.

This particular question of armaments as cause of wars includes one especially crucial point : the Anglo-German naval competition. This was perhaps one of the chief causes of England's entry into the war, but certainly not of the war itself. Speaking as we are of its aims we could dismiss this point even without consideration. No responsible man in England has ever formulated any intention of including in the peace terms a clause preventing Germany from further increase of her navy. Of course there was, and there is still, a hope that engagements on the sea will result in a *de facto* réduction of the strength of the German fleet. But from this hope to the view that a

Power of seventy million inhabitants can be " forbidden " ship-building is a long way, and so far we have no proof that anybody here intends to press this special point at the peace negotiations. So we have the right to leave this question out. Still let us remember that it presents the same pros and cons of the greater controversy of armaments. Naval militarism is, after all, a sub-division of general militarism. The one can no more than the other be made directly responsible for conflicts between State and State. Here again we have only a weapon which serves warlike purposes but does not create them. Two strong naval Powers can live in peace side by side indefinitely just as two strong military Powers, unless contending interests force them to draw the swords—or to weigh the anchors. Of course an international agreement for mutual limitation of naval armaments would be a very useful reform just as in the case of land armaments. But it would be risky to think that the time has already come for such an arrangement on land or sea. It is not likely that peoples, all conscious of the mighty resources within their grasp, would willingly renounce using them. It is the same psychological impossibility that we should meet if we advised a healthy youth to abstain from sport under the pretext that he may become too strong and thus dangerous to his neighbours. We do not think that the innate human tendency to develop one's full strength is likely yet to be bound. It is much easier to deal with the contending interests : they *are* the causes of wars, and they *do* admit practical settlements which are within the boundaries of real life, not within those of Utopia.

*   *   *   *

Thus it is to the contending interests that we have to return in our search for the root of the present evil. Of those, we have already seen that none either of the western or the northern ethnical problems, was ripe enough or bad enough to provoke the European war ; and, in consequence, none of them is likely to provoke a new conflagration even if this one leaves their settlement to future times. So we are forced to turn our minds and eyes, once and for always, to the Near

East. A closer examination will show us that the manifold contending interests knotted here could not have been untied in any other way but by war ; and that, in consequence, should the present war leave them tangled as before, they would inevitably lead to another.

III—ASIATIC TURKEY

III

Asiatic Turkey

Everybody, of course, remembers that the European war originated from events in the Near East : the crime of Serajevo, the Austrian ultimatum to Serbia, Russia's desire to defend her natural ally in the Balkans. And yet it seems sometimes as though we have forgotten it. Since August, 1914, other developments filled the foreground ; and even the Gallipoli campaign did not restore the Near East to its due place in the public's attention. It almost looks as if the circumstances which preceded the Russian mobilization had only been futile accidents, mere pretexts used and then deservedly dismissed. It is time to remind ourselves that it was not so. We say remind, because surely it is only a question of temporary distraction, not of ignorance. Whoever has any notion of politics knows that the death of the Archduke Franz Ferdinand was a consequence of the old Austro-Serbian tension, that the Austro-Serbian tension was a result of a phenomenon called "Drang nach Osten," and that the Drang nach Osten is the greatest driving force in the Balkans. This point need not be explained—simply recalled.

What has to be explained is the geographical meaning of the term Near East. The Near East which has magnetized the lusts of nations for ages and still magnetizes them now, is not Serbia, not Albania, not Macedonia—it is Asia Minor. Our immediate attention for the last years has been too much absorbed by the little, though bloody, struggles of little Balkan peoples, and we forgot that the real problem of the Near East is a problem of Western Asia, not of the Balkans. The Balkans may constitute the final aims of Greece, Bulgaria or Serbia ; for the Great Powers, whose relations determine the destinies of the world, the Balkans are nothing more than an antechamber leading somewhere else. Put in plain words the Near East question is the question of the partition of what remains of Turkey.

"Drang nach Osten" is a term generally applied to both Austria and Germany. Let us begin with Austria. Is her "Drang"

circumscribed to the Balkans, do her
dreams end at Salonika ? What is Salonika by itself ? A little provincial town
of 150,000 inhabitants with an annual
harbour trade of some £2,500,000 in imports and some £1,200,000 in exports.*
It cannot justify the historical policy of
a Great Power, unless we admit that the
Great Power saw and sees in the possession
of the small town only a starting-point
for a further push.† Look at the Austrian

---

* *Cf.* Trieste with £47,750,000 imports, £42,300,000
exports ; Smyrna with £3,725,000 imports, £5,722,000
exports.

† " Salonik ist eine Zukunftshoffnung. Dereinst,
wenn Vorderasien der Kultur erschlossen, wenn die
Eisenbahn Mesopotamien durchziehen und der Per-
sische Meerbusen durch einen Schienenstrang mit
Smyrna verknüpft sein wird, dann wird Mazedonien
als Durchzugsgebiet für den grossen Ueberlands-
verkehr zwischen Mitteleuropa und Vorderàsien wohl
zu neuer Blute emporsteigen, und Salonik zu grosser
Bedeutung gelangen."—(Leopold Freiherr von Chlum-
ecky, " Oesterreich-Ungarn und Italien," 1907, p. 233.)

exports : they prove that the focus of Austrian interests, even commercial, is in Asia Minor and Syria, not in the Balkans. Look at the admirable organization of the Austrian Consular Service in Western Asia, at the elaborate system of education which prepares officials for this service ; look at the programmes of the commercial academies in Vienna and Budapest which include much more Arabic and Turkish than Serbian or modern Greek, and care much more for the geography of Anatolia and Mesopotamia than for that of Albania or Thrace. These facts speak with a clear tongue. No matter whether we can or whether we cannot find in books, articles or speeches of Austria's leading men direct hints pointing to ambitions which go beyond Salonika. Even for ambitions pointing to Salonika such literary evidence is not abundant. Acts are more eloquent than words or absence of words. Even admitting for a moment that Austria would politically stop at Salonika we see the prospect unchanged. From this harbour Austria would overflow Western Asia's ports with her own and German products and thus cut a thoroughfare for both herself and Germany. Austrian and German policy in the Orient has always been considered as one and the same thing, Austria playing the part of propeller on tracts which were beyond Germany's immediate reach. Be it for herself or for her ally, Austria coveted the borderless spaces and the bottomless resources of Asiatic Turkey, not the strip of second-rate land leading to a third-rate coast town on the Ægean.

The case of Germany is even clearer. Here there is no lack of plain words either. Beginning with Moltke and up to Professor Hasse, the Pan-Germanists have always pointed to Syria, Palestine, Anatolia, Armenia, even Mesopotamia as to future German dominions.* In the well-known series of Pan-Germanist pamphlets published by Lehmann in Munich under the general heading " Kampf ums Deutschtum," a special issue written by a good specialist has been dedicated to these ambitions. It dwelt especially upon the

---

* *Cf.* The excellent book of Mr. P. Evans Lewin, " The German Road to the East," 1916.—Mr. Barker in the *Nineteenth Century*, June, 1916, produces the following list of authors who at different times advocated the idea of " Deutsch Kleinasien " : Wilhelm Roscher, Friedrich List, Paul de Lagarde, Lassalle, Rodbertus, Karl Rittel, Moltke, Ernst Hasse, Dehn, Rohrbach, Sprenger, Sachau, von der Golz, Kaerger, Nauman, Schlagintweit. . . .

value of the German colonies in Palestine
and Anatolia as forerunners of the coming
German rule. Another pamphlet of the
same series wore the suggestive title:
" Germany's claim on the Turkish heritage " (" Deutschlands Anspruch an das
Türkische Erbe ").* To these full-mouthed

---

* Other suggestive titles: Amicus Patriae, " Ar-
menien und Kreta—eine Lebensfrage für Deutsch-
land," 1896 ; Dr. Karl Kaerger, " Kleinasien, ein
deutsches Kolonisationsfeld," 1892. We read in
this pamphlet : " Nicht Hunderte und Thausende,
nein, Millionen von Kolonisten können hier eine
zweite Heimath finden "—and, in order to get
Turkey's permission for such a flood, the author
suggests that Germany should, in recompense, guar-
antee Turkey's integrity " gegenüber fremden
Angriffen."—A. Sprenger, " Babylonien, das reichste
Land in der Vorzeit und das lohnendste Kolonisationsfeld fur die Gegenwart," 1886. M. A. Chéradame
quotes from this book the following lines which we
give in his translation : " De toutes les terres du
globe il n'y en a pas invitant davantage à la colonisation que la Syrie ou l'Assyrie. . . . Si l'Allemagne
ne manque pas l'occasion . . . elle aura dans le
partage du monde acquis la meilleure part." The
same French writer quotes from the famous review

manifestations we can add the Kaiser's journey to Palestine in 1898. Before the war we used to treat as nothing such pamphlets and visits. Now we have seen that what pamphlets said and visits foreshadowed Governments really meant and were preparing for. Some people tried even to deny the political intention underlying the colossal project of the Bagdad railway: recent events, we hope, have told them the truth. Germany was perhaps not exactly aiming at the partition of Turkey, because she would prefer to swallow Turkey as a whole.

Alldeutsche Blaetter, number for 8th December, 1895 : " L'interêt allemand demand que la Turquie d'Asie, au moins, soit placée sous la protection allemande. Le plus avantageux serait pour nous l'acquisition en propre de la Mésopotamie et Syrie et l'obtention du protectorat de l'Asie Mineure habitée par les Turcs."—(A. Chéradame, " Le chemin de fer de Bagdad et les puissances," pp. 5 and 7.)

TURKEY AND THE WAR

The French claim on Syria, the British on Mesopotamia, the Russian on the Straits and Armenia, the Italian on Adalia, Greece's pretence upon Smyrna, and some other similar demands will be partially dealt with in the last part of this book. Here it is enough to mention them. They give us, in conjunction with what we have said of Austria and Germany, a whole net of political wills and tendencies converging to the same end : destruction of Turkey.

It is mere commonplace to say : Austria sent the ultimatum to Serbia because she wanted to get nearer to Salonika. But if we look deeper we at once disclose what this commonplace means. Austria sent the ultimatum to Serbia because she wanted to get nearer to the Turkish heritage in Asia Minor. The real cause of the Austro-

Serbian conflict was the problem of further partition of the Ottoman Empire.

It is mere commonplace to say : Russia wanted to shield Serbia because the little Slav kingdom was her main fortress in the Balkans. If we look deeper we see at once why Russia wants fortresses in the Near East. She wants them because of her need to push towards the warm seas, through the Straits or through the mountain chains of Armenia. The real cause of the Russo-Austrian conflict was the problem of further partition of the Ottoman Empire.

It is mere commonplace to say : Germany wanted to shield Austria because Austria was her only reliable ally. Were it only for this reason, then it would have been much easier for Germany to advise

Austria to settle the Serbian conflict in some peaceable way. Germany chose the other more dangerous course, because she wanted Austria to conquer the little Slav kingdom. Why? The answer is given in the now fashionable battlecry: Berlin to Bagdad. The real cause of the Russo-German conflict was the problem of the future domination of Asia Minor.

Now it would be, of course, an exaggeration to say that France and England have also been involved in the war because of their respective " claims upon the Turkish heritage." The immediate considerations which forced France to abide with her ally and Great Britain to join them were surely of quite another nature. But this fact does not affect the truth upon which we insist. When once the whirlpool sets in movement, it is natural that boats passing within the circle of its force should be caught into the maelstrom. What matters is to discover the thing which started the vortex. Just in the same way, had the initial conflict arisen because of Alsace, Russia would probably have been driven into the war, though she has nothing to do with this particular question. But Alsace did not and could not generate the initial conflict. It was born in the Near East by the peculiar problem of the Near East, and this fact is the essential feature of the whole situation.

That is not all. The problem of the "Turkish heritage" is one which can be settled only by war. Alsace-Lorraine constitutes only one thirty-sixth of the German territory, the Italian Irredenta is

not more than one-sixteenth of the Haps-
burg Monarchy. Their separation from
their present owners would not mean
destruction of the Central Empires. If one
day, by some unforeseen influences, perhaps
by a good bargain, Germany or Austria
could be persuaded to cede these provinces,
it would not mean their suicide. Whoever
is sanguine enough to believe in the miracles
of progress may also believe in the possibility of this miracle. With Turkey the
situation is different. The " claims " cover
more than three-quarters of her present
area. No optimist in the world can dream
of a peaceable settlement for a litigation
of such character and size. Here it is no
question of bargain, cession, arrangement :
it is a question of " heritage." To leave
a heritage the owner must die.

IV—PARTITION AND WAR

IV

Partition and War

Is it, however, inevitable that the old owner's death should be accompanied by a fight between the heirs? Can we not imagine a joint European action against Turkey based upon a previous compact which should allot to every Power its fair portion of the estate, thus excluding any danger of a second European war? Could not the successful experience of the *first* Balkan war be repeated on a greater scale? To this question, sad to say, we must reply with a doubt. Let it never be forgotten that the first Balkan war was followed by the second, and the lesson of *this* experience is perhaps much more human than the other. The claimants on Turkey's future spoils are England, France, Russia, Germany, Italy, perhaps Austria, then also Greece and Bulgaria. Even forgetting for a moment that they are divided into two hostile camps, it needs too much imagination and optimism to admit the probability of an agreement conciliating such a host of different wills in such a delicate matter. When Venizelos succeeded (and only for a moment) in bringing three little Balkan Powers to a mutual accommodation in a question touching historical national lusts, he was proclaimed a genius; and yet his task was so much easier because the little Powers felt very dubious about their own capacity to kill the Bear, and it is known that such doubts make people more conciliatory. When they saw the bearskin in their hands the conciliatory spirit vanished and the only voice heard was that of greed. For a " concert " including all the great European Powers the acquisition of the bear's skin would be a sure and easy job; that is why the voice of greed would be loud from the very beginning. Where is the genius able to conciliate half a score of mighty appetites under these conditions? Germany looks to Bagdad with the same insistence as England; Armenia and Kurdistan, claimed by Russia, are at the same time included in the most popular schemes of " Drang nach Osten "; Constantinople is coveted at least from three different sides. And what about Turkey herself? She would never submit to lie still and "wait and see" how her neighbours conspire against her: she would conspire herself, she would make alluring offers to one of them in order to keep him apart from the others; she would complicate the game, mix the cards and render a general concert impracticable, even if it were feasible by itself. The partition of Turkey can only be a result of a European war, not of a concerted European expedition.

Some soft-hearted people may perhaps ask: But is it not possible for all these great Powers to renounce their claims on Ottoman property? We believe that it is humanly impossible. Of course the world knows instances of renounced and forgotten claims. The best example is

the Italian indifference to such parts of
the Terre Irredente which are under French
or Swiss rule. Corsica speaks an Italian
dialect ; Savoy is the cradle of the dynasty
which united Italy ; Garibaldi was born
in Nice and bitterly resented her non-
inclusion in the young State which he
more than helped to create. To-day all
those vindications are more than forgotten : they are dead, dead in Italy as
well as in Corsica, Nice and Savoy. The
canton of Ticino is Italian in tongue and
Swiss in soul, and no Italian Nationalist
dreams of annexing it. There is a powerful force in the world known by the much
abused name of Culture. This force secures a State's dominions better than any
wall of bayonets. Culture is impervious.
Where its fertilizing presence is felt, where

it constantly produces higher standards of life and work, where it unceasingly causes all the vital energies to play, all the germs to grow, there a foreigner's claim, meeting no echo, is soon stifled, worn out, drowned in indifference on both sides. What excites and feeds again and again a neighbour's greed is the emptiness and lifelessness of waste ground that could be turned into gardens, the consciousness of rich possibilities which the present owner is impotent to exploit. It has something to do with the old belief that Nature abhors a vacuum. The push towards cultureless spaces is humanly irresistible. Their desolation itself is a constant provocation. That is why the thirst for the " Turkish heritage " can never die—except through satisfaction.

And it can be satisfied in no other way but through war. That is how the present conflict was born. That is why, if this war leaves Turkey undivided, a new war of the same size will follow sooner or later, with the inevitability of the tide.

PART II—THE INNER STATE OF TURKEY

V—AFTER SIX YEARS OF CONSTITUTION

V

AFTER SIX YEARS OF CONSTITUTION

IT is a painful duty to insist upon the destruction of a living body. It is especially painful for a writer who knows the people he dooms to death. If there are good peoples and bad peoples, the Turks certainly belong to the first sort. As a rule they are honest, modest, hospitable, chivalrous. Their ancient glory as soldiers stands in spite of all. They are fine statesmen—of course for conditions which are no more. It is hardly possible to get in touch with them and not to love them. If politics could—or should—be based upon sympathy, nobody would like the idea of destroying an Empire founded and maintained by these nice fellows. Unhappily politics are based upon other factors.

The whole world hailed the Young Turkish Revolution of 1908 in the sincere hope that a new era of real progress had opened before the Ottoman Empire. On the eve of the Great War the disappointment was general and for ever incurable. Experience has clearly shown that there was practically no difference between the Old Turkish and the Young Turkish régime. The Parliament, almighty in the early days of the Revolution, was reduced to practical slavery. The administration was as bad as in Abdul Hamid's days. The condition of the Christian races " improved " only in as much as they were admitted to compulsory military service ; but the most precious stronghold of their national existence, the communal and educational autonomy which even Abdul Hamid had respected, was made a target for menaces and attempts. Never had the Old Turk tried to interfere with the national individuality of his non-Turkish subjects : he was indifferent to the language they spoke at home or in school. The Young Turk did not hide his object of gradually imposing his language upon Arabs, Albanians, Armenians, Greeks and Slavs of the Empire. Bribery in office, muddle and corruption in court showed no promise of disappearing—rather the opposite. The Albanians, the most loyal of Ottomans in former days, were driven

into revolt by stupid governmental pro-
ceedings. The massacre of Armenians in
Adana left nothing to desire for one who
remembers the high standards of the
massacres of 1894–1896; and the Young
Turkish Government left the official cul-
prits unpunished like the Old Turkish.
Against all this not one step, not one act
of any progressive character can be written
on the credit side. We mean progress in
any sense—political, social or economic.
The obsolete laws ruling the tenure of land
are still unchanged in spite of all efforts,
although they constitute the greatest
obstacle to the economic development of
the country. Mortgage of rural properties
is still practically impossible, and so no
sound system of agricultural credit can be
created. The recognition of the " persona

juridica," indispensable condition to a free immigration of foreign capital, is still a pious wish.

It has been said that the Young Turkish Government " had no time to do things." This is an exaggeration. The constitutional régime was consolidated in the early summer of 1909 ; the Tripoli War began only in the autumn of 1911. Two years are sufficient to show a good will and a fair understanding. Of course nobody pretends that the Young Turks could have *carried* out social reforms in two years ; but it is an awful exaggeration to say that such reforms could not have been passed in Parliament. They were not even proposed. Whoever witnessed in those years the life of the Ottoman Chamber will attest that it had plenty of time to legislate ; but the time was spent in futile intrigues behind the curtain. Was it lack of patriotism ? Certainly not. Was it lack of statecraft ? Perhaps. But first of all the cause of this innate impotence of the " new " régime is to be found in the organic construction of the Turkish Empire.

Before we deal with this organic defect of the country it will be of some use to throw a glance upon the men. We said, just now, that one of the reasons of the failure was perhaps lack of statecraft. Let us shortly recall the essential features of the human element known by the name of Young Turks.

VI—THE YOUNG TURKS

VI

The Young Turks

THE morning after the Turkish Revolution everybody in Constantinople, Salonika, etc., was " a Young Turk," " a member of the Committee," a Somebody or a Something in the then victorious conspiracy. But the real Young Turks who prepared and carried out the Revolution were not numerous. They formed two distinct groups : we shall describe them roughly as the Young Turks of Paris—and those of Turkey.

When we say Paris we mean not only the French capital but also London, Geneva, in general all the western towns where

Turkish emigrants used to concentrate in the long days of Hamid. Paris was the main centre. Here Ahmed-Riza published his organ, the " Meshveret," in two editions—the Turkish one for his fellow-countrymen in the distant homeland, and the French one for Europe. Here Prince Sabaheddin conceived his own programme of Ottoman reconstruction which included in a rather unexpected combination the two battlecries of decentralization and private initiative. The few members of the Liberal Turkish intelligentsia who were lucky enough to get permission to go abroad, used to make their pilgrimage to Paris as to a kind of political Mecca. Even those among the emigrants who lived in England or Switzerland drew their political wisdom only from Paris. It is useless for us to inquire why they chose France—of all the European countries the most unlike their own—to be the school and the model of their constitutional lore. Enough to know that it just happened so, and that in describing the Young Turkish emigrants as a Paris group we point not only to a geographical fact but also to the main factor which influenced their intellectual development.

France is a strongly centralized country, uniform and ruled by a uniform system which is applied everywhere in the same way. There are even Frenchmen who think this uniformity too exaggerated. But it is a consequence of a past disease —of the excessive provincialism which divided and sterilized France before 1789. Every province was almost a different state, with different laws and taxes; it was not uncommon to talk of a "nation Normande," "nation Picarde," or "nation Auvergnate." The great Revolution had before it the task of amalgamating them all into one nation. That is why it insisted upon the principle of uniformity and centralization with such emphasis that even now the average French politician recognizes in them one of the holiest dogmas of 1789, one of the main assets of freedom and progress. The Young Turks imbibed these ideas without any criticism or discrimination. They knew that the greatest misfortune of their own country was also the fatal disunion of the different elements of population; and they conceived the naïve belief that the remedy which saved France would be equally fit to save Turkey. It seemed to them that differences between Turks and Armenians, Greeks and Bulgars, Serbs and Albanians were to be taken and treated in the same way as differences between Normans and Picardians. Thus was born and rooted their deep enthusiasm for the system of centralization and assimilation. Sabaheddin, with his confused programme which admitted a shadow of local distinctions, remained in a hopeless minority. The Armenian Revolutionists tried several times to persuade the " Meshveret " party that the only system fit for a constitutional Turkey is that applied in Switzerland or at least in Austria—system of provincial self-government and national autonomy. But the Young Turks abhorred their scheme, and so it came, towards the end of the 'nineties, to a definite break between the followers of Ahmed-Riza and the Dashnaktzutiun.

Such curious political aberration implies of course a tremendous ignorance of the real conditions in Turkey. And ignorance it was. The Young Turks were not the first example of emigrants who lost in exile every feeling of the realities in the Motherland. We have instances of no lesser miscomprehension in the schemes and tactics of the Russian Revolutionists who tried to " lead " from abroad the popular movement of 1905. Their mistakes showed how deeply they ignored the most essential facts of Russia's intellectual and social life. Yet Russia was not an unexplored country like Turkey is; they had at their disposal exact statistics, mono-

graphies dealing in a scientific way with
the different problems of the country, a
highly developed monthly and daily Press,
a constant intercourse with tens of thousands of educated Russians travelling
abroad. The Young Turks of Paris lacked
all that. For long, long years they were
practically cut off from any living touch
with the *milieu* which they struggled to
free and revive. Visitors from Turkey
were rare, shy and uninformed. No wonder
if they gradually lost all sense of possibilities, distances and proportions.

This reproach could not be fairly applied
to the other group—the Young Turks in
Turkey. These were humble, poor fellows
living in the everyday life, little post clerks
like Taraat, schoolmasters like Djavid,
soldiers like Enver. They worked among

the masses and knew them thoroughly. They fully realized the deep gulf fixed between the various races which hated each other in Macedonia and Armenia. They knew their own country. But this was the only thing they knew. It must not be imputed for blame to a person brought up in Turkey if we admit certain gaps in his education—or even if in some cases we consider his whole education as one big gap. Hamid's system of censorship was ideal in its own way—it was impenetrable. The Young Turks in Turkey were doomed to ignore many things which are written in books. But the thing about which their ignorance was really fabulous was one that cannot be learnt from books. This thing was—Constitution. Its blessings and its failures can be taught only by

life itself, by life in a constitutional country.
Peoples accustomed to Parliaments and
responsible Governments know that a constitution is not the solution of difficult
problems—it is only the way through
which the contending forces of a country
can search for settlements of problems.
They know that a constitution means
growth and development of internal
struggles, not pacification. For a people
living under tyranny the constitution is
a dream, perfect and absolute as only
things in dreams can be. It is the con-
ciliation of all the dissensions, settlement
of all the quarrels, it transforms enemies
into brothers and hate into love. Such
was the political dream of the Young
Turks in Turkey. Well they knew how
serious was the clash of conflicting interests

between the different nationalities of their country ; but firm and strong was their belief that there is one magic remedy and its name is Constitution.

So the two groups represented two different types of misinformation. Those in Paris were acquainted with the lights and shades of representative government, but they did not know the country to which it had to be applied. Those in Turkey knew the country, but had a queer idea about the omnipotence of a parliamentary régime. With a little good luck the two groups might have been the complement each of the other. The Parisian Turks might have contributed their knowledge of constitutional life, the local workers their acquaintance with local realities. It might have made quite

a valuable combination of statesmanship.

But the Young Turks had in this sense
bad luck. Their misfortune was the too
easy victory of the revolutionary movement. In a fortnight's time, without a
shot, without any bloodshed, they became
the rulers of Turkey. Easy victories are
dangerous. They make people too confident, frivolously sanguine, inclined to
believe in the practicability of every dream.
Such was the atmosphere when, the day
after the Revolution, the two groups met
after long years of separation. Instead of
amalgamating their truths they amalga-
mated their mistakes. The combined programme included a Parisian ignorance of real
Turkey and a childish belief in the miracu-
lous almightiness of " The Constitution."

Do you remember the Arabian tale of the ingenious association of the blind and the legless ? The blind man took the legless man on his shoulders and the trust thus formed had at its disposal one pair of good legs and one pair of good eyes. In the case of the Young Turks the opposite happened : the legless was entrusted to carry and the blind to lead.

We saw them at work. The spirit which permeated the average Young Turk resulting from this amalgamation is best shown by a living portrait. We choose for such purpose one of the most influential and of the least known leaders of the " new " Turkey. His name is Dr. Nazim. He is a rare and curious personification of both types. He was a student of medicine in Paris, but for some years before the

Revolution he worked among the masses under heavy risks and privations. The legend tells that, when troops were sent from Anatolia to Salonika to crush the revolutionary movement, Nazim-bey, disguised as a "kaffedjee" (coffee seller), managed to get on board the military transport—and, when the ship reached the rebel town, officers and soldiers were all under his influence. Even if exaggerated this tale shows the man. After the victory he became, behind the curtain, the soul and the gist of the Committee "Union and Progress." He declined all offers of ministerial posts, even of a seat in Parliament. While streams of gold were pouring, from all sides, into the coffers of the Committee—and also into some individual pockets of the Committee—

Dr. Nazim, the chief secretary, accepted
only a ridiculously modest monthly pay—
people said, about five or six Turkish
pounds. His working day oscillated between 16 and 20 hours. He never ap-
peared in public, but everybody knew
that " Dr. Nazim is the Committee."
And in truth by his strong will, by his
cold fanaticism, by his unbending one-
sidedness he influenced all the policy of
the Young Turkish headquarters between
1909 and 1912. His speciality, his strong
point, was of course the main problem of
Turkey—the racial problem. His point
of view in this question was very simple :
he denied its importance. He was persuaded that differences of language, national
habits, etc., are only a sham doomed to
disappear by the mutual consent of all

the races in the Ottoman Empire. They needed such distinctions only so long as they had to struggle against tyranny. " Once freedom is proclaimed and everybody has equal rights, they will be only glad to throw away their superfluous foreign tongues in favour of Turkish. As a matter of fact, you see, it is not Turkish —it is the Ottoman language." Dr. Nazim was sure that Arabs, Greeks, Armenians would accept this programme without any serious reluctance. The opposition to it would be limited to small factions of worn-out leaders, most of them in the secret pay of foreign Governments. The bulk of the people would be sensible, they would overthrow their former nationalist chiefs and follow the call of " Ottomanization." Does not the same thing happen in all the constitutional countries? About this last point, too, Dr. Nazim was absolutely sure. He "knew from the best sources" that in free countries racial questions do not exist. And Austria, Hungary, Belgium, Canada, Ireland, Switzerland? "Oh, tout cela n'a pas d'importance," Dr. Nazim used to reply, imperturbably. Besides, his great hope was Socialism. He was sure that this movement would soon develop into Western proportions (and that in a country where the first industrial factory, so to say, was yet to be created). And he "knew from the best sources," that the Socialists fight everywhere against the conservation of local idioms in favour of the one and indivisible language of the one and indivisible State. His conclusion was: "Les nationalités? nous les digérerons toutes."

These were not the ideas of one individual. As we said, they inspired the Young Turkish policy which led to the revolts in Albania, to the loss of Macedonia, and to the loss of what was far more precious than any portion of land—the loss of trust.

But, in fairness to the Young Turks, we must repeat : the main cause of their failure was elsewhere. Had they been wise as Solomon and wily as Macchiavelli they would have failed all the same.

VII—THE TURKISH MINORITY IN TURKEY

VII

The Turkish Minority in Turkey

The essential feature of the Ottoman Empire is the fact that its ruling nation, the Turks, is a relatively small minority of the population. Precise statistics for Turkey do not exist, but it can be assumed that out of the roughly estimated 21 million inhabitants of the Empire on the eve of the war, 7 million were Turks, 9 million Arabs, 1½ million Armenians, 1½ million Greeks, 1½ million Kurds, the remainder Jews, Druses and smaller tribes. The ruling race was only one third of the whole. Yet we must remember that this is the most favourable proportion ever attained in Turkish history. A hundred years ago the Ottoman Empire embraced the whole of the Balkan Peninsula, with Roumania and Bessarabia, Bosnia and Herzegovina, Cyprus and Crete and all the Isles of the Archipelago, Egypt, Tripoli, and, at least nominally, the better part of what is now the French Colonial Empire along the Southern Mediterranean coast. In that Greater Turkey the Turks were perhaps one sixth of the population. Yet they not only conquered that colossal area—they kept it and ruled it through centuries. Such an achievement could not be performed by the bare strength of sword. It implies also a great deal of true and wise statesmanship. The old Sultans were mighty warriors and clever rulers—clever, of course, in their own way. But they had naturally to pay a heavy price for the keeping of their Empire. The small Turkish race was forced to concentrate all its energies on two objects : war and government. Peasantry as the natural storehouse of vital forces of the race, soldiers, and officialdom—these three elements form the whole structure of the Turkish nation. The heavy burden of defending and running the State's machine made it impossible for them to develop a commercial, industrial, or intellectual middle class. This fact is at the bottom of all the decisive events of Turkish history past and present.

Of course the world knows other and even modern instances of Empires where the ruling nation is a minority. The best example is Austria (apart from Hungary). Its German population is only 37 per cent. of the whole, but this minority still dominates the country. In spite of the fact that paragraph 19 of the Austrian Constitution establishes complete equality of all the racial elements and all the languages, the German tongue is still de facto the true " Staatssprache," and the Germans, although they have no numerical majority in Parliament, constitute the overwhelming element in Government and bureaucracy. It would be unjust to suppose that such predominance is simply the result of abuse of power. It is rather a natural consequence of the real superiority of the German factor in various provinces of social life. The German culture as a whole is of course stronger than that of the

Poles, Czechs or Ruthenes; the level of
individual culture is also far higher with
the Germans than with any other element,
and we can say that the Austrian
intelligentsia is two-thirds German. The
material wealth is also accumulated, from
days immemorial, in German hands. The
industrial capital in Austria—even if we
speak of Bohemian or Galician industries—
is almost exclusively German. So are the
great majority of industrial staffs. The
organized proletariat—one of the main
factors of Austrian political life—is also pre-
dominantly German. The same statement
must be repeated speaking of Austrian commerce, inner and international. Last but
not least—the big landowners, the feudal
lords whose influence is felt in that country
not less than in Prussia, is thoroughly

German, with the exception of Galicia and a part of Bohemia. Thus the German element prevails in the life and in the politics of Austria owing not so much to State's protection as to its own real weight.

It will be useful to compare this state of things with the position of the Turkish element in Turkey. The comparison will be highly instructive.

Take the cultural side. In Austria the Germans are unquestionably the leading factor in this respect. Their language is understood in the whole Empire not because it is forced upon the people, but because it is indispensable for both intellectual and economic life. The Turks can hardly boast any such natural privilege. Of all the races in the Ottoman

Empire which possess any culture at all, the Turks are the last and the weakest.

Their culture has no right even to be mentioned in comparison with the bottomless riches of Hellenism.

The Arabs possess a great old civilization, a mighty literature which constitutes practically the only base of the scanty intellectual wealth of the Turks. The literary Turkish is so permeated with Arabic words that, not only in books dealing with learned matters, but even in simple newspaper leaders nearly all the nouns are generally Arabic.

The little Armenian nation invented its curious alphabet in the end of the fourth century of the Christian era. Its old literature is comparatively very rich ; its modern literature, which includes also translations of almost everything that is valuable in European knowledge and fiction, is incomparably above the Turkish standard. It is an unforgettable merit of the two Mehitarist monasteries, in Vienna and Venice, that even in the worst times of Armenia's last century they never interrupted their patient work of compilers, translators, and publishers. The Armenian press is up to good Russian standards, a praise that means a lot. Their theatre, without being first-rate, still does exist, while the Turkish stage is so far practically a mere project.

Before the severation of Macedonia, Turkey had numerous Bulgarian and Serbian subjects, who again had no reason to look upon the Turks as their superiors or even their equals in matters of culture.

TURKISH MINORITY IN TURKEY

The Ottoman Jews, with the exception of those in Palestine, have no national culture in the modern sense, but they are educated in French schools, read French books and newspapers and would consider " turquisation " as a sort of degradation. The only peoples over whom the Turks can really claim cultural superiority are Albanians and Kurds.

The most unfortunate feature of this humiliating position of a ruling race is the fact that all the subject nations are receiving a constant intellectual support and impulse from abroad—Greeks and Slavs from their respective kingdoms, Arabs from Egypt, Armenians from Russian Armenia, etc. The only race which has no intellectual centres beyond the frontier are the Turks. Quite opposite to this is the condition of the Austrian Germans. They are only 10 million, but their civilization is the product of 60 million Germans who live outside Austria—while their main opponents, the Czechs, have nobody to support them from abroad.

The consequence of all this is the insignificant part the Turkish language plays in the Turkish Empire. In the Arab provinces it practically does not exist: nobody knows it, nobody minds it. But even in Constantinople it has hardly any importance outside of the pure Turkish quarter of the town. In commercial relations French and Italian are predominant, Greek very useful, Turkish hardly ever heard. The non-Turkish educated class very seldom knows enough Turkish to read a book, and hardly ever enough to write a decent letter. "As a rule a Christian in Stamboul knows Turkish only if he is an Armenian or a lawyer," said an observer, and his word can be taken roughly as the truth. The Armenian community on the Golden Horn had been forced to learn Turkish by horrible persecution in Hamid's days; of the other races, not so cruelly tried, only those rare individuals need to know Turkish who come in constant immediate touch with Turkish courts or governmental offices. Otherwise there is no need of Turkish in Turkey.

In the economic life the Turkish element has no part or significance whatever. Of course there are about 6 million Turkish peasants; and among the small shopkeepers and lower artisans we find a good many Turks. But in the somewhat higher grades of economic activity we find none. In the sea-borne trade, which constitutes in Turkey the main source of wealth and social influence, no presence of Turkish capital or mind can be traced. The capital is mostly foreign, the personnel partly foreign, partly Greek, Armenian, Jewish, Syrian, or Arab; and most frequently it is recruited from that mixture of all European races which is called the Levantines. A Turkish clerk is indeed a rarity. Also in the few existing embryos of Ottoman industry—mines and tobacco—the capital is foreign, the staff entirely non-Turkish.

It is true that the big landowners in Anatolia are mostly Turkish pashas and beys, and so it was in Macedonia. But those " feudal lords " cannot be compared with their prototypes in Austria. The mighty landlords of old Europe are tied by innumerable bonds to their hereditary estates, to their peasants, to the population of the neighbouring towns and suburbs. From grandfather to grandson they were looked upon as patrons, protectors, or tyrants of their shires; they lived in their castles, they were loved or feared, they left indelible traces on every page of local history. Tradition and social intercourse, not the bare fact of ownership, give them that tremendous specific weight which makes the political strength of the feudal class—in our instance of the feudal class in Austria. The Turkish landlord has, as a rule, nothing to do with his estate. The " djiftlik " is mostly alloted to the meritorious official or general as a reward or a favour; the owner never saw it, is not likely ever to see it, will certainly not pitch his tent amid its primitive wilderness. The estate is administered, or to be more exact, is bled, by a manager, and so even the hatred of the villagers is limited to the servant without reaching the master. To be sure, there are exceptions, but this is the general type of big landownership in Turkey. It is a source of revenue, not of influence. It is almost as impersonal as an investment in foreign shares.*

---

* " When speaking of the Turks of the higher class, it is well to remember that there are no wealthy men in the European sense among them. Nor is there any class of nobles. There are no great families proud of their descent, and possessing historic estates. . . . In Turkey there are no ' country houses,' no Moslems or even Christians who display wealth in the villages."—(Sir Edwin Pears, " Turkey and its People," 1911.)

VIII—ILLUSIONS AND DISAPPOINTMENTS

VII—ILLUSIONS AND DISAPPOINTMENTS

VIII

ILLUSIONS AND DISAPPOINTMENTS

THESE are the conditions with which one has to reckon if one wants to realize how hard a task it is to keep the Turkish rule in Turkey. A small minority in numbers, they have not even the comfort of being, as our often-mentioned Germans in Austria, a *relative* majority : whilst, against 10,000,000 Germans, there are only 6,435,000 Czechs, 5,000,000 Poles, etc., in the Ottoman Empire the Arabs outnumber the Turks. The Turkish culture is one of the poorest in Turkey, their language is one of the least considered ; their part in the higher levels of economic life is little short of nothing. Peasants, soldiers and officials, they rule the country only as long as they are able to keep the sword and the seal in their hands. Their authority is not supported by any fact of the life outside the barrack and the office; it is built upon itself alone and can only last as long as every seat representing any infinitesimal fraction of power is kept by a Turk.

The conclusion is clear. Turkish rule in Turkey can be assured only by autocracy, and rather a mediæval autocracy. When we say mediæval our intention is to point to the well-known fact that absolutism in the middle ages meant practically much more individual freedom than for instance *" l'absolutisme éclairé "* of

the eighteenth century. The latter en-
deavoured to interfere with every detail
of private or municipal life. The former
cared for recruits, taxes, obedience—and
nothing else. Such was the system of
the Old Turkish Sultans, taken as a whole
and apart from exceptions. The Old Turkish imperial formula was : " sovereignty,
power, politics are *our* exclusive business ;
the inner affairs of the non-Turkish communities are *their* own exclusive business."
So the Old Turk kept every thread of
political power jealously in Turkish hands.
But he despised and avoided, as a rule,
every meddling with the communal, ecclesiastical, or scholastic affairs of his Christian
and Jewish subjects. They enjoyed a kind
of communal autonomy which ought to be
studied even for purposes of modern legis-

lation. Every non-Mahommedan nationality throughout the Empire was considered as a legally constituted and organized " millet " (Turkish for " nation "). There was the " millet-i-rum," including all the Greeks of the Ottoman Empire, " millet-i-bulgar " for the Bulgarian schismatics, " millet-i-ermeni " for the Armenians, " millet-i-moussevié " for the Jews. Every millet was ruled by a representative body, called " Medjliss," *i.e.*, Parliament, or Diet, and a spiritual Chief, Patriarch or Exarque, or Chief Rabbi. The ecclesiastical titles must not mislead us : the functions of these dignitaries were far from being purely ecclesiastical. The Chief was the acknowledged legal representative of his millet before the Sublime Porte in all political matters. On the other side he was the constitutional leader of his " nation." The organization of the little " parliaments " was sometimes very interesting. The most complete of all those miniature constitutions was the so-called " Sahmanadrutiun " —the Statute of the Armenian community, passed law in 1862. It included elaborate provisions for the election of members of the medjliss. The latter was divided into two boards—one for purely ecclesiastical affairs, one for the secular matters of the community. These secular matters embraced a very wide province of civil life : education, hospitals, charity, marriages, divorces, questions of heritage, dowries, etc., transfer of real property from one member of the community to another. Such wide inner autonomy was especially valuable in matters of education. The schools, elementary or higher, belonging to the different communities, were free from any interference of the Government : they chose by themselves their language, programme, school books, and teachers. In numerous schools, where even foreign languages were taught, the teaching of Turkish was completely neglected. The Old Turk did not care a snap for it. "Speak what you like and learn what you prefer, only do not interfere with my State's power," was the basic principle of his political wisdom.

Then the Young Turks came, and "ils ont changé tout cela." On the one side they introduced a constitution which admitted non-Turks to the control of State's affairs. On the other side they showed an unquestionably keen intention to interfere with the inner affairs of the up-to-then autonomous communities. Their formula was : " We meddle in your business and you meddle in ours." It was quite the opposite of the old system—the old system which kept the Ottoman Empire through centuries, because it left to the subject races an illusion of freedom in the things that were most sacred to them. The new system frightened and exasperated them by its menace to get under the thumb of the State the last remnants of their national life ; it made of them even more implacable foes of the Ottoman idea than before. At the same time it handed to them a big share of the State's power !

A Parliament is supposed to reflect the co-relation of the social forces existing in

the country. Those social forces are constituted not only of numbers of men
belonging to the different groups of population. Their respective wealth, culture,
the part they play in the vital branches
of the country's activity—all these count
not less than bare numbers. Votes are
not simply counted—they are weighed
says a modern political proverb. Here in
Turkey everything was against the Turks
—numbers, culture, economic rôle. However, they managed to secure something
like a Turkish majority at the first elections
owing to the unpreparedness and disunion
of the Christian races, the disorganization
of Arabs and Albanians. But it soon
became clear that at the following elections the numerical and economic predominance of the non-Turkish elements

would inevitably find its expression in the structure of the Parliament.

In the beginning of the constitutional era the Young Turks overlooked this perspective. They were yet under the spell of the illusion which we have just described—the illusion of the coming " ottomanization " of the non-Turkish races. At that moment they were, or sincerely believed that they were, utterly and thoroughly democratic. We remember the outburst of their indignation when, in 1909, Damad Ferid, one of the Senators, proposed to strengthen the constitutional powers of the Crown. His argument was that, owing to the overwhelming predominance of non-Turks, the only asset which was and would remain Turkish for ever was the Osman dynasty: therefore, the State's power should be vested rather in the unchanging Crown than in the unstable Parliament. This Senator happened to be a Damad— the Sultan's son-in-law. His proposal was generally attributed to this delicate relationship. The Young Turks unanimously refused to accept his point of view. The objections then formulated on their side had a frankly republican accent. Even ecclesiastical members of the Lower Chamber declared that it was against the spirit of the Koran to strengthen the throne. Two years after, the Damad's argument became the keystone of the whole Young Turkish policy. In December, 1911, when Saïd Pasha introduced a bill enlarging 'the Crown's rights for dissolution of the Chamber, Ahmed Riza showed, as president of the assembly concerned, the most unexpected energy in checking every attempt of opposition to this measure. Before the outbreak of the Tripoli campaign—*i.e.*, before the beginning of the systematic destruction of Turkey—the republican coquetries were entirely forgotten and the Young Turks represented what they are now—a purely monarchist, nationalist, conservative party. They abhor every idea of real political progress, not because they like inertia, but because in Turkish conditions progress means liquidation of Turkish rule in Turkey. Life, the great Counsellor, forced them to return to the old wisdom of the Old Turks.

IX—"EST DELENDA"

IX

" EST DELENDA "

THIS natural fear of progress is not only felt in political matters. It can be said without exaggeration that it became the main spring of the whole Young Turkish system, applied even to problems of a purely economical character. The absence of a Turkish commercial, industrial or intellectual middle class means that any step forward in the economical development of the country must inevitably result in enriching the non-Turks and consequently in weakening the Turkish element. This fatality lends a dangerous political

135

flavour to the most harmless enterprises, such, for instance, as creation of electric tramways or building of harbour-quays. What is the use of it since directors, officials, clerks, engineers, foremen will inevitably be Greeks, Armenians, Jews, Levantines, if not foreigners altogether? It had been thought that the Old Turk's instinctive dislike of introducing foreign capital in Turkey was caused only by fear of international complications. Now in the case of the Young Turk we see that it was and is rather the apprehension of inner complications.

We have repeated the word fatality several times. Let it not pass unnoticed or be taken for a mere rhetorical ornament. The progress of Turkey is a thing of objective impossibility. After all, the Revolution of 1908 was not the first attempt to open the gates of progress to the Ottoman Empire. Midhat Pasha was once a greater Liberal than any of the Young Turkish leaders of to-day, and he was surely a great and wise statesman ; and even before Midhat's time the important reforms of 1839 and 1856—the so-called Tanzimat— were unquestionably inspired by broad liberal ideas. The Tanzimat resulted practically in failure, and Midhat's career in tragedy. It would be naïve and short-sighted to attribute these miscarriages simply to personal attitudes of Sultans or to intrigues of Ambassadors. Nor can they be fairly ascribed to the influence of Mahomet's law. Did Islam prevent the mediæval Arabs from becoming the leading race of western civilization ? We sometimes hear travellers and journalists talk of a "negative spirit of Islam." It is a mistake. A great religion, whatever be its minor errors, is always a positive and a constructive driving-force, unless it becomes a weapon in the hands of a Power which has negative interests. Such a Power is the Ottoman Empire. The Ottoman Empire : not the Turkish race. Were the Turks, so to say, left alone in the limits of a strictly-national State, without the burden of ruling a huge majority of other races, they would unquestionably have shown themselves second to none in that corner of the world where the standards of modern culture are kept by Bulgars and Roumanians. They would have developed a quite decent commercial and professional middle class ; they would have created an industry, a literature, a theatre of their own. But fate, glorious and tragic, made of them gardeners in a garden too big for their resources. So it inevitably became their only concern to prevent grass from growing, buds from flowering—if possible, sun from shining. This was their only way to keep, somehow, the colossal household from overgrowing, throttling and ejecting its masters.

Optimists may ask : is there no possibility of a change in the Turkish psychology? Could they not make up their minds to submit to the inevitable loss of their own dominating position in Turkey for the sake of Turkey's unity? Could they not give in to the necessity of their own submersion by a flood of non-Turkish elements for the sake of the preservation of an Ottoman Empire that would be Ottoman no longer ? To all these questions everyone who has any understanding of what is called a nation's soul will find only one reply : No, never. Ruling races hardly submit to such transformations even where the change evolves slowly and gradually. Since it became evident in Austria that the growth of the Slavs menaced, though in a remote future, to undermine the dominating part which belonged to the German element, the German Nationalists lost every interest for the conservation of Austria's unity. On the contrary, they began to look for a possible reduction of Austria's size in order to carve out a country not so vast—but with a solid German majority. Their programme of 1882—so called " Das Linzer Programm "

—asked for the " Sonderstellung " of Galicia, *i.e.*, for exclusion of the main Slav province from the number of the " kingdoms and lands represented in the Reichsrath." Their battlecry was, as an ironic verse put it, " Das Vaterland soll kleiner sein "—let the Fatherland be smaller. This is the natural attitude of a ruler who has to choose between loss of power and reduction of his State's boundaries. Unless he is a saint—which peoples never are —he will prefer to remain the chief in a village rather than to become one of the crowd in Rome. Old Turks or Young Turks, they will never accept the perspective of an Ottoman Empire where the power of the Turkish race would be reduced to a share proportionate to its numerical, economical, and cultural nullity. Shall this be the reward and the result of centuries of glorious military exploits and wise statesmanlike decisions which made the names of so many Sultans and Viziers immortal ? The Turks—Old or Young— will try their utmost to prevent this national catastrophe ; and, as the only way to prevent it is to block the natural evolution of the vital forces of the country, that is what they will do.

Turkey under Turkish rule is doomed to remain backward, unenlightened, barren. This doom is irremovable so long as the Ottoman Empire shall last, and its heavy burden crushes and condemns to death every spiritual bud that sprouts from either Turkish or non-Turkish stalks. The destruction of the historical absurdum called the Ottoman Empire will be a blessing for both Turks and non-Turks. The latter, independent or placed under protection of mighty civilizing Powers, will freely develop their long-subdued vitalities ; the former, liberated from the oppressive load of Imperial responsibilities, will enter an era of peaceful and productive renaissance. He who wishes Turkey's destruction is a friend, not a foe of the Turkish race.

PART III—CONTROVERSIAL POINTS OF THE PARTITION SCHEME

X—A LIST OF CLAIMS

X

A List of Claims

THE purpose of this introductory chapter is simply to recall the extent of the various territorial claims which have any serious chance to be considered in the emergency of the coming dismemberment of the Ottoman Empire. We say to recall, and this term marks the exact limits of our present task. We are not prepared to try to explain all such claims, to defend them, to support them : our object consists mainly in, so to say, drawing a map of the existent aspirations. To discuss whether the reasons and interests upon which they seem to be founded are valid in every case is beyond our intentions. Such discussions are, as a rule, useless and in the majority of the cases impossible. The arguments generally employed to support territorial claims are mostly as hard to refute as to prove. Is, for instance, the presence of French-speaking inhabitants a sufficient reason for the establishment of a French protectorate ? It is and it is not : it is in the case of Beyrouth, but it is not in the case of Salonika or Constantinople, although French is much more frequently spoken in the two latter towns than in the Syrian harbour. Or, to take another example, does the existence of invested Italian capital constitute a fair base for Italian annexation ? It certainly does for Valona, but it would not for Syria, although, from a pure economical stand-point, Italy's capital is much more in-terested in Syrian than in Albanian enter-prises. What matters is the will of a great nation to expand in a given direction : interests, reasons, arguments, historical - recollections, religious senti-ments and what not are only of secondary importance.

In one case only does it seem to us advisable to call the reader's attention to the real interests involved in the issue : when the situation shows germs of a controversy between the Allies themselves, or between Allies and neutrals. To make a comparison between two contending claims is much easier than to give a plausible proof of the absolute well-foundedness of one. We only know of two instances where a unanimous agreement between the Allies (although attained and secured between the Governments) is not fully realized by the public. One is the fate of Constantinople and the Straits. It has been ascertained from reliable sources that the Entente Cabinets have arrived at a full mutual understanding on this secular problem; but public opinion in England and Italy does not yet seem sufficiently prepared to welcome the solution foreshadowed by the Allied diplomacy in accordance with the vital interests of Russia. The second question which is still unsettled so far as uninitiated circles are concerned is the delimitation of French and English spheres of influence in Syria. It seems that a complete and satisfactory agreement in this matter has been reached at one of the Paris Conferences ; but here again public discussion in both France and England remains behind the progress realized by their own diplomatists. To these two questions we will dedicate special chapters.

In connection with the problem of Syria's future another question arises which, in days to come, is bound to play a prominent rôle in Eastern politics. It is the question of Arab national aspirations. The Governments do not seem very much concerned with this movement as yet, and indeed it looks as if they were right in refusing to attribute any exaggerated importance to a promising but unripe phenomenon. What an observer*

* André Dubosq, " Syrie, Tripolitaine, Albanie," 1914.

recently said seems to be true and recognized as true by all those who know the Orient : " What is prematurely called ' the Arab movement ' is as yet not more than the expression of local tendencies with no concordance between them. The Yemen, the Nedjed, Bagdad, and Syria are not on the eve of marching under the same flag to the conquest of an Arab supremacy." The ordinary public, however—we mean of course that part of the public who know of the existence of such a thing as an Arab Nationalism—may be sometimes inclined to feel puzzled at the seeming contradiction between European and native interests. We try to point out some aspects of this interesting problem in one of the following chapters.

Another and the last chapter will deal

with the German claims on the Turkish heritage. We think that victory, however complete, must not relieve the winning side of the obligation of reckoning with the vital necessities of the conquered foe. Of course, we are not going to advocate a " generous treatment " of the " crushed " German Empire—this would be ridiculous in dealing with an enemy who will be beaten but never crushed, and who will never require nor accept generosities. But the interests of a durable peace would be irrevocably compromised were Germany excluded from—at least—commercial expansion in the Orient. At the same time, the rights of the Turkish race must not be forgotten ; and it would be only fair to every side concerned if both claims, Turkish and German, could be settled by one and the same arrangement.

Another national problem is connected with the settlement of Palestine's fate. The Jewish question has been brought into special prominence by the horrible sufferings of the Russian and Galician Jews in the war-zone, and the fact that the Government responsible for these sorrowful events is an Allied Government makes of this question a debt of conscience for the Western members of the Entente. At the same time various manifestations of the Zionist idea, especially the one which took the form of a " Zion Corps " attached to the British Expeditionary Force in Gallipoli,* called the attention of the

---

* Lt.-Col. J. H. Patterson, " With the Zionists in Gallipoli," London, 1916.

A LIST OF CLAIMS

English public to this old undying hope, to the endeavours of the Zionist Organization, and to the existing Jewish colonies in Palestine. But we do not think that this problem, however "actual" it may be, and whatever may prove its importance for the future of the Near East, belongs naturally to the special category with which we are now dealing. It has no immediate and necessary connection with the question of delimitation of frontiers. The Zionist aspirations tend not so much to full independence—at least for the present—as to a sort of "Charter" including guarantees of self-government and privileges for colonization. Such a Charter could be granted, theoretically speaking, by any liberal government, be it French or English.

For the remainder we shall confine ourselves to a bare recital of the main revin-
dications formulated by the Allies or
friendly Powers, officially or unofficially,
in connection with the present war.

England seems to include in her aspired
zone of influence the whole of Mesopotamia and the Southern part of the Syrian
coast land, including probably also the
control over the corresponding portion
of the Hedjaz railway.

The French zone of aspirations embraces the whole of Syria including Alexandretta in the north, Damascus and
Aleppo in the east, and Palestine in the
south ; the last claim, however, seems to
have been abandoned in deference to British
interests.

Russia demands the possession of the

Straits ; this implies the annexation of
Constantinople and the adjacent part of
the present vilayet of Constantinople on
the European side of the Bosphorus, as
well as of Scutari and surroundings on the
Anatolian side ; further, the possession of
all the islands in the Sea of Marmora, of
the Gallipoli Peninsula and of the Asiatic
coast of the Dardanelles. Russia also
claims control over the whole of historical Armenia, embracing the vilayets
of Erzerum, Van, Bitlis, Kharput (Mam-
uret-el-Aziz), and Diarbekir. As an alternative to the annexation of the Straits it
has also been spoken of leaving to Russia
the ancient region of Cilicia, corresponding
to the present vilayet of Adana ; this
would evidently imply the possession of a
fairly wide " thoroughfare " leading from

Adana-city in this region to Kharput in Armenia.

Italy claims control over the ancient region of Pamphylia—the present Adalia in the vilayet of Konia. It is also a matter of common knowledge that Smyrna began to attract, during the last years, a good deal of attention from official and commercial Italy.

If Greece joins the war on the side of the Entente, Smyrna, and probably the whole vilayet of Aidin which forms Smyrna's " hinterland," will be claimed by this Power on the ground of important ethnical affinities and serious commercial interests. Greece will also insist on having a share in the future control of Constantinople and Gallipoli.

Roumania, even having joined the war on

our side, does not seem to have any positive claims on the Turkish heritage ; but she will countenance the annexation of Constantinople to Russia only under some arrangement securing a strong representation of Roumanian interests.

XI—THE STRAITS

XI

THE STRAITS

CONSTANTINOPLE is claimed by Russia, Greece and Bulgaria. The part Bulgaria has chosen in this war does not fit her for the rôle of a pretender to a town which belongs to one of her allies. The partition of Turkey implies a victory of the Entente, and we can hardly imagine such victory resulting in a reward for Bulgaria. Besides, the Bulgarian pretence is not backed by any serious argument of either ethnical or economical character. Constantinople has no more than 15,000 inhabitants of Bulgarian race and speech, out of a total

M

population of 1,125,000 ; another 10,000 could be found perhaps in the environs of the city. The commercial interests of Ferdinand's kingdom have been completely settled since the conquest of Dedeagatch : Bulgaria possesses what is denied to Roumania and to Russia—an ice-free port on the right side of the Straits. The Bulgarian claim on Constantinople is a rare example of a political pretence absolutely void of any plausible justification, being an outcome of mere ambition and mania grandiosa.

The Greek case has much better foundations. It may be questioned whether the so-called historical rights have any practical value in our prosaic days ; but it is undeniable that the historical rights on Byzantium can be claimed by none but

Greece. In addition Constantinople has a Greek population of 'more than 200,000, who play prominent parts in every vital branch of local life. That is no small matter—but that is all. Greece cannot support her claim by any argument showing on her side a real practical need for Constantinople. Her maritime position is ideal without the Golden Horn. And even the racial argument cannot be accepted without objection. A town or a country can be claimed on purely ethnical grounds only if the majority of the population belong to the claimant's race. This is not the case in Constantinople where the Greeks are only one-fifth of the inhabitants. So the only title which indeed cannot be questioned in itself is the historical right as aforementioned. It is a great factor, but it can hardly stand against a claim based upon vital economical interests.

Such is Russia's claim. Its unpopularity with the English public must be mainly attributed to the fact that it was always considered as a mere product of Panslavistic ideas. It may be true psychologically or it may not : we leave it undiscussed because it really does not matter. Whatever may have been the motives of him who first formulated " Byzantium for Russia " and of those who supported or inherited this battlecry, it is now strongly supported by people who have nothing to do with Panslavism. Even if there were no Slavs at all in the Balkan Peninsula, or if Russia were not a Slav but a Latin or a Chinese Empire, its push towards the Straits would remain what it is—a natural and obvious necessity.

We hardly think it worth while to indulge in proving this commonplace truth. A look at the map would be sufficient, even if the well-known events of the war had not previously brought this fact to the consciousness of every impartial observer. Still a few figures may be useful to recall some experiences in the good old days of peace—experiences which were in their own way not much sweeter than those of war-time. Russia's export of cereals amounted in 1910, for instance, to 847,100,000 pounds, of which more than a half were forwarded through the Black Sea and Azov Sea ports. The part which these ports play in Russia's shipping traffic can also be seen from the following distribution of tonnage (entered and cleared) between the three sea-shores of European Russia in the same year, 1910 :

			Entered. Tons.	Cleared. Tons.
White Sea	-	-	-	830,000	829,000
Baltic Sea	-	-	-	5,547,000	5,629,000
Black and Azov Seas		-	7,555,000	7,424,000
Total	-	-	13,932,000	13,882,000

Thus more than a half of Russia's exports is under the absolute and unlimited control of the ruler of the Straits. Worse than that : Russian commerce depends upon the goodwill not only of the Turk but of any of his innumerable enemies, big or small. Every complication in the Near East is bound to result in the closing of the Dardanelles. So in the three years preceding the war the Straits were closed twice. The result can be clearly shown by figures illustrating the effect which the Tripoli and Balkan wars had on the Russian exports. The grain exports sunk from 847,100,000 pounds in 1910 to 547,900,000 pounds in 1912 ; the shipping traffic in the Black and Azov Seas decreased from 7,555,000 tons entered and 7,424,000 cleared in 1910 to respectively 5,712,000 and 5,575,000 in 1912. What it means for Russia can be seen in the instance of Odessa. The two successive closings of the Straits resulted in completely shattering the economic health of this once flourishing town. Since then Odessa is visibly declining, and many of Russia's leading authorities on trade matters doubt whether she will be able to recover from her wounds.

We do, however, notice even now a

strong instinctive aversion in the average English mind to Russia having Constantinople and the Straits. It is time to insist upon a fair and thorough revision of this almost hereditary feeling. We insist upon it not because Russia is Britain's ally, but because a durable peace can only be built on bases which will satisfy the vital necessities of each among the great leading Powers. The British public must realize once and for always that a State of Russia's size and resources cannot be indefinitely held away from the ice-free sea. The new ice-free haven on the Murman coast, now completed and connected with the main Russian railway lines, will be not more than a provisional remedy good for war-time, *faute de mieux;* but it is of no value as a permanent solution. It is situated in the interesting region of the famous midnight-sun, so dear to the hearts of the Scandinavian poets : that is to say, it has plenty of sunlight by day and by night in the summer months, when this port is not needed, and no sunlight at all, even by day, just in those winter months when the other havens of Russia are ice-bound. Imagine Liverpool being compelled to perform all the operations of piloting, loading and unloading at night-time only, and ask any expert whether it can be considered as a relief for a country of Russia's magnitude and riches. In addition, the Murman port is a port in a desert—in a desert that is doomed to remain a desert for all eternity. Such a port is an absurdum. And even a bigger absurdum is to think that the Russian

Empire can declare itself satisfied with this makeshift. Russia will strive for the free sea in spite of the world's and her own pacifist tendencies, impelled by irresistible necessity.

Her way to Port Arthur was barred eleven years ago by the events of Liaoian and Tsushima, and everybody in Russia is definitely reconciled to the idea that it is barred for ever and that the attempt was itself a mistake. So there are only three ways for Russia. She must look for a free sea port either on the western coast of Norway, or on the southern coast of Persia, or on the Mediterranean. Geography does not allow of any other choice.

Let the British public think over this choice, having in mind not Russia's but Britain's interests. Should Russia be compelled to look for a footing on the Scandinavian coast, it would mean a Russian base just facing the British Isles, and not even too distant from the Firth of Forth. Sven Hedin, the famous Swedish traveller and the intellectual leader of Swedish "Activism," said, among too many exaggerations, one sensible thing : he showed that, if Russia chose to establish herself on the Norwegian coast, the northern fjords of Norway—Narvik for instance—would be of no use to her for the same reasons which depreciate the Murman port —midnight - sun and desert. In Sven Hedin's opinion Russia would then prefer some harbour on this side of the Polar circle, blessed by darkness at midnight and sun at midday all through the year and leading into a populated country :

Trondheim, for instance. This Trondheim is only 648 nautical miles from the Firth of Forth. Of course we firmly believe in the complete harmony of Russian and British interests. But the balance of forces in the North Sea is already such a delicate and complicated thing that many common-sense Englishmen will prefer it to remain as it is without further complications.

The alternative is, as we said, a port on the Persian Gulf. This perspective, we suppose, is even less alluring to English opinion. Instead of explaining why, let us repeat the good French proverb: *A bon entendeur, peu de paroles.*

From the British point of view the solution which means the least inconvenience or apprehension for the future is to see Russia established on the Eastern

Mediterranean. The Mediterranean Sea is an open sea leading freely to any part of the world's ocean. But God and History shaped it into a form very convenient to British Imperial interests. The way to India from the Mediterranean leads through the Suez Canal which is controlled by Britain, and the way to the British Isles from the Mediterranean leads through the Straits of Gibraltar which are also controlled by Britain. We refuse to admit that England's past policy towards Russia was ever inspired by the desire to prevent the free development of her natural maritime possibilities. We interpret the shade of diffidence, felt and expressed on this matter by the English public in days past and forgotten, as a legitimate anxiety to keep the control of the seas in the hands of a

nation to whom sea-power means everything. We choose to believe that even
in those days English opinion would gladly
have agreed to any settlement conciliating
Russia's right to an access to the free sea
with England's natural jealousy of the
ocean. The Dardanelles solution serves
both purposes in a most admirable way.

We use, indiscriminately, the names
Constantinople and the Dardanelles because they express the same thing. The
possession of the Golden Horn would be
of no use without that of Gallipoli. Timid
people suggest the compromise of sub-
mitting the Bosphorus to one rule and the
Dardanelles to another. But what is the
good of free traffic through the Bosphorus
if the Dardanelles shall remain liable to
be closed as before at the least shadow of

a quarrel in which Russia has nothing to say ? The possession of the Straits implies the possession of both passages on both sides, Anatolian and Roumelian, including Constantinople and Scutari, Princes' and Marmora Isles, Gallipoli and Dardanelles-city.

We do not see why this scheme should be considered an odious annexation clashing with the principle of nationality, holy to the Allies. This principle, as already said, can be fully applied only where there is a clear and decisive predominance of one race, in numbers as well as in cultural value, over the others. Such is by no means the case of the territories indispensable to assure Russia's control of the Straits. Here is an approximate, but reliable, statistical estimate of the main elements of the population in the region including Constantinople with its Asiatic dependencies (the suburbs of Kanlidja, Scutari, Kadikeuy, the cazas of Princes' Isles, Ghezbé, Beykos, Kartal, and Shilé), the sandjaks of Chataldja and Gallipoli, and the mutessarriflik of Dardanelles :

Turks - - - - - -	600,000
Greeks - - - - - -	325,000
Armenians - - - - -	200,000
Levantines - - - - -	75,000
Jews - - - - - -	70,000
Bulgarians - - - - -	30,000
Foreigners - - - - -	130,000
Total (including smaller groups) -	1,450,000

This motley composition absolutely refuses to support any claim based on ethnical grounds. The Straits cannot be annexed to a State " of their own race " because they have no race of their own. Their destinies can only be discussed and decided

from the standpoint of economical necessity and political efficiency.

Of course we know that a strong party,
especially in Roumania, suggests a compromise : neutralization of the Straits and
of Constantinople. At the first glance this
project seems alluring as all compromises
do ; but, as almost all of them, it is an
utterly inefficient scheme, bound to create
a precarious and dangerous state of things.
Russia needs a passage completely and
absolutely free, independent of the good
will of her neighbours, big and small, near
and far. What neutralization means, the
world has learnt on the first day of this
war. This lesson will never be forgotten.
The " neutralized " Straits could be seized
and occupied in spite of scraps of paper
before Russia could oppose it by force,

and all that would remain to her would be the moral comfort of writing diplomatic notes. Would England ever agree to a neutralization of the Suez Canal without having secured for herself the control— the military control—of its approaches? The situation at the Dardanelles is quite analogous. Even more : the Suez Canal after all is not the only way to India, whilst the Dardanelles are indeed the only access to Russia's South. Some international agreement concerning the free use of the Straits may prove indispensable and would certainly not be opposed by Russian opinion in principle ; but Russia could accept it only as a corollary in a settlement which should leave to her the full sovereignty, the military and administrative control of the two shores of the Bosphorus and of the two shores of the Dardanelles.* Any other decision of the half-way sort would inevitably lead to this one result : that Russia would seize the first opportunity to help herself out of a precarious " neutralization " which would leave her, just as now, under the sword of Damocles. On the other side, there is no need to complicate the question by alleging that, in order to secure her future position on

---

* The *Rech* of Petrograd, the leading daily of the Constitutional-Democratic Party, wrote in 1915 : " With the idea of neutralization the discussion is not yet closed for us. . . . The forms and degrees of neutralization can be extremely various, from that applied to the Strait of Magellan to that of the Panama Canal where the United States has the right to raise fortifications just for the security of the Canal. . . . If this problem has been settled for Panama, there is no reason to think that it could not be settled with the same success for the Bosphorus and the Dardanelles."—(Quoted, in a French translation, by M. N. Dascovici, " La question du Bosphore et des Dardanelles," 1915, p. 293.)

the Straits, Russia must claim an uninterrupted land approach from Batum to
Scutari. England and France keep their
over-sea dominions without land approaches. The Russian Black Sea fleet,
under future conditions, will be completely
equal to the task of connecting the little
colony to the great metropolis.

XII—SYRIA AND PALESTINE

XII

Syria and Palestine

If we eliminate the Drang nach Osten, France has practically no competitors as far as Syria is concerned. True, Colonel Churchill wrote in the 'sixties that Syria is geographically and historically the indispensable corollary of Egypt, and that both ought to belong to England. But, although one-half of this prophetic wish has been fulfilled, we think that nobody in Britain would press for the execution of the second moiety.

If such a tendency can be discovered anywhere in our days, it is perhaps among a section of Arab Nationalists in Egypt and Syria. Their argument may be worth mentioning. It presents a new feature in the development of Arab political opinion. Until recent times the Arabs, especially those of Syria, were understood to be strongly Francophil—inasmuch as they did not consider the possibility of complete independence. It was a natural result of their education, as most of the modern-taught Arabs passed through the numerous French schools of Syria. But since the beginning of this war several symptoms pointed to a notable change in this attitude, at least among a section of Syrian leaders. One of them, who lives in Paris, gave us the following explanation of this new departure.

" Before the war broke out it had always

been an axiom with us that England did not want Syria. So the only alternative to Turkish rule, for those who did not believe in independence, was France. The Turkish menace to Egypt changed the whole situation. My friends from Cairo write me that now on all sides the conviction is growing that England will not be able to remain indifferent to the future of Syria. They think England will claim for herself the southern part of the Syrian coast, if not the whole of it. If it is true, then we Arabs have to reconsider our attitude. If we really have a choice between France and England, many of us would prefer England. We do not feel any particular love for either ; as a matter of feeling, our instinctive sympathy goes rather to the French than to the English.

But the French rule is centralistic and tends to impose on the native population the French language and customs. England is incomparably more liberal. We have two examples before our eyes : Tunis and Egypt were occupied at the same time. Tunis has been completely " frenchified " in everything — administration, tribunals, schools, even religious education ; whilst in Egypt our national language plays a prominent rôle in schools and public life. This difference is eloquent enough. Besides, there is another consideration of no less importance. The populations of the southern and eastern Mediterranean coasts, who all speak Arab dialects and could form in the future a great united nation, have been cut up into sections under different rule : Morocco, Algeria and Tunis are French, Tripoli is Italian, Egypt is British, and now they are speaking of Syria about to become French. I think it is *trop de morcellement.* Many of us will certainly prefer Egypt and Syria to be one, under the same rule, and so to constitute a powerful nucleus of Arab nationhood." *

---

* *Cf.* also the impressions of a French observer close at the eve of the war : " De toutes les puissances qui cherchent à étendre leur influence sur la Syrie et la Palestine, l'Angleterre est avec la France la seule vers qui aillent les aspirations des populations désireuses d'échapper de quelque manière au gouvernement des Turcs. . . . Sans vouloir mettre en doute la bonne foi du gouvernement anglais lorsqu'il déclara l'année dernière n'avoir ' ni intention d'agir, ni dessein, ni aspiration politique dans ces régions,' il n'en est pas moins vrai que les musulmans se tournent vers lui et qu'il ne fait rien pour les décourager. Certes, aucune propagande officielle n'est faite par l'Angleterre en Syrie, mais il faut que les musulmans aient été, comme on dit, fortement ' travaillés ' précédemment par ses agents pour qu'ils la regardent comme leur protectrice naturelle. On vit au printemps dernier les notables musulmans reclamer au

These ideas did not 'pass unnoticed. In the early spring of 1915 they formed the subject of a lively polemic between some leading vernacular papers of Cairo. A little later, one of the most important Paris dailies spoke with some anxiety of "a section among the Syrian Arabs who are said to turn their eyes towards a Power other than France," and tried to persuade them that France is still the fittest alternative for them.

We think that this last opinion is entirely shared by all responsible men in

---

consul d'Angleterre à Beyrouth aide et assistance contre les autorités ottomanes, et les journaux de France épiloguèrent longuement sur l'incident. Que les diplomates anglais n'agissent plus aujourd'hui sur les musulmans de Palestine et de Syrie, il n'en reste pas moins que l'Angleterre a conservé sur eux une influence politique dont ils sont devenus eux-mêmes les propagateurs."—(André Dubosq, "Syrie, Tripolitaine, Albanie," 1914, pp. 32, 33.)

British politics and press. The only question that remains and really concerns vital English interests is to know where the southern frontier of the future French Syria should be drawn.. In other terms : Syria must unquestionably go to France, but what shall be the fate of that southern part of the Syrian coast which bears the historic name of Palestine ?

This question has met with little interest on the part of the British public, with the exception of some official circles in this country and in Egypt. Not so in France. The question of Palestine is vividly discussed in papers and at public meetings ; the battlecry is " *il nous faut la Syrie intégrale.*" Among the leaders of this propaganda we find many prominent names— for one instance, that of Senator Leygues.

Although not in the least supported by the Government, which keeps a correct silence on the whole matter, this movement shows that French political sentiment is almost as keen on Palestine as on the rest of Syria.

Analysing, however, this part of the French claim, one cannot help seeing that it is hardly supported by anything but sentiment. Palestine occupies less than a sixth of the total surface of Syria, and includes less than a sixth of Syria's total population. In the present conditions it is the poorest part of Syria. The large commercial towns, Beyrouth, Damascus and Aleppo lie outside of Palestine; compared with them Jerusalem is small and poor. Palestine has no natural harbour comparable to Alexandretta or Beyrouth. And indeed commercial arguments do not play any noticeable part in the agitation in favour of a French Palestine, whilst they predominate in any *exposé* of the French case concerning the rest of Syria. The case for Palestine is supported exclusively by motives of an ideal sort, such as recollections of the first Crusade when Godfrey of Bouillon and Baudoin of Flanders founded the kingdom of Jerusalem, doomed to disappear in one century, or the tradition which from 1535 and 1604 to 1878 entrusted to France the protection of all the Christians in the Orient and particularly of the pilgrims going to the Holy Places.

It would be cynical to underrate the value of ideal motives. Supposing that after the partition of Turkey there could arise a question of entrusting the " protection of Christians," or the guardianship of the Holy Places, to one Power, no nation would be better entitled to perform this honourable task than France. But the protection of Christians has been assumed long ago by all the Christian Powers for their respective dependents, reducing the French privilege to practically nothing.*

---

* M. Delcassé said in the French Chamber, on January 19th, 1903 : " Le protectorat de la France (*i.e.* the protectorate over the Christians in Turkey) ne s'étend pas ; il s'étend de moins en moins à des étrangers. Depuis quelques années, il a évolue. Tout en gardant son caractère universel (?), il tend de plus en plus . . . a ne s'exercer qu'en faveur des Français et à leur bénéfice exclusif."—(Quoted by M. A. Chéradame, " Le chemin de fer de Bagdad et les Puissances," 1903, p. 309.) " C'est surtout depuis le traité de Berlin que les droits de la France furent contestes et battus en brèche. . . . Le protectorat, ce n'était plus, en effet, comme jadis, la protection des marchands et des pelerins, chaque nation se chargeant aujourd'hui de protéger les siens. On pouvait meme contester qu'il fût question des ordres

Besides, such protection was needed only as long as Palestine was under Mohammedan rule. The partition of Turkey will remove this state of things purely and simply, leaving no ground even for the slightest fiction of ex-territorial protection. Whichever be the State that will inherit Palestine, it will be just as able to protect Christians as England in Egypt or France in Tunis.

---

religieux latins, des évéques latins, etc., puisque l'article 62 reconnaissait a chaque puissance le droit de protéger ceux de sa nationalité. On pouvait soutenir que le protectorat ne consistait plus que dans les prerogatives honorifiques . . . " " Dans ces trente dernières années, c'est la volonté du Saint-Siège qui empêche notre protectorat de s'effriter sous les efforts de nos rivaux. Mais aujourd'hui la France a rompu avec le Saint-Siège ; il peut en résulter, un jour ou l'autre, l'abandon formel ou tacite des instructions de 1888 et de 1898 ; ce jour-là le protectorat, dans sa forme ancienne, aura vécu."— (René Pinon, " L'Europe et l'Empire Ottoman," 1905, pp. 553 and 568.)

But the essential point which removes the foundation itself of France's ideal argument is the question of guardianship of the Holy Places. In this matter it would be idle and dangerous to cherish any illusions. To avoid confusion, the strictest distinction must be kept in mind between Palestine as a whole, and the Holy Places in particular. The latter include a large part of Jerusalem, Bethlehem, Nazareth, and two or three minor localities. No arrangement is thinkable leaving them in the hands of *one* Christian Power. France in her Orient policy was and is a Roman Catholic Power. It does not seem that even Protestant States would like, or simply tolerate, the establishment of her one-sided control over cities and villages considered as the common

property of all the Christian Churches.
But there is certainly one Power which
would oppose such a solution with all its
energy, and that is Russia. Militant Orthodoxy, jealously exclusive — especially
in its relations to the Roman Church—
is an avowedly prominent factor in
Russia's inner and foreign politics. The
keen interest for the Holy Places shown
by the Russian Church is a well-known
fact, and it is supported by the unparalleled numbers of Russian pilgrims annually
flooding Jerusalem at Easter time. So far,
however, official Russia has shown no sign
of political intentions as regards Palestine ;
she is not one of France's competitors for
this portion of the Turkish heritage. But
any attempt to bring the Holy Places
under the rule of a Roman Catholic Power

would provoke very undesirable complications. We can scarcely imagine anything so likely to imperil the harmony of the Entente as the idea of a French Holy Sepulchre. This idea is impracticable, and we understand that it has already been dropped. The Holy Places will form a group of enclaves governed by an international commission.

Nothing remains then of the ideal value which the possession of Palestine could have for France. The two glorious titles which make the fascination of the " crown of Jerusalem "—protector of Christians in the Orient and defender of the Holy Places—have been irremediably cancelled by time and the force of events. What remains is the memory of the short-lived Crusaders' kingdom of seven hundred years ago. Is it enough to nourish a steadfast enthusiasm for the idea of " Syrie inté- grale " ? And is it enough to counter- balance the heavy, the really vital military reasons which force expert observers on the English side to recognize in Palestine the natural bulwark of the Suez Canal ?

As we said, this truth is only slowly filtering through the minds of this country. We remember having read, a little more than a year ago, the following lines in the *Fortnightly* : " . . . It is difficult to ima- gine any British Government voluntarily assuming such a burden (protectorate over Palestine), unless as a proved military necessity, and no one can seriously main- tain that proposition. The desert may not be an impregnable frontier, but it is at least a formidable one, and the line of the Suez Canal is much easier defended than any frontier that could be drawn between Palestine and Syria. . . . It has always been British policy to avoid, wherever possible, having land frontiers coterminous with those of great military States."*

The author expressed a view very common at that time, and not altogether forgotten even now. It is worth closer consideration. The Sinai campaign, though poor in events, is rich in lessons. In the following we quote a letter dealing with these lessons, written by a foreign journalist who witnessed the engagements on the Suez Canal in February, 1915.

"I am afraid you in England confuse two things: the defence of Egypt and

* J. B. Firth, "The Partition of Asia Minor," *The Fortnightly Review*, April, 1915.

that of the Suez Canal. The former, of
course, is secure—but not owing to the
desert. The desert did not prevent the
enemy from approaching El-Kantara and
Serapeum. But for the Canal, he could
have approached Zagazig as well. What
protects Egypt is the Suez Canal, and
not in the least the desert. I admit that
the Canal is an impregnable barrier : but
then you must consider it only as a means
of defence. That is what your generals
do. But can you forget that the Suez
Canal is by itself a value which must be
protected ? I always thought that the
Canal was the only reason why England
chose to keep Egypt—that its value for
England is much greater than that of
Egypt. Now you treat the Canal simply
as a first-line trench, or an outpost of the

Egyptian fortress. First-line trenches and advanced outposts are susceptible of being seriously damaged even by an enemy who is too feeble to take the fortress itself. So it is in the case of the Suez Canal. An enemy having Palestine for his base is hardly likely to penetrate into Egypt; but are you sure he is not likely to make your Canal useless and impracticable for the whole time of the hostilities?

" I fear that it is not only possible but even easy. The depth of the Canal is 11 metres (12 yards); its width on the surface varies between 80 and 120 metres (88–132 yds.); but the width which is more important is that at the bottom, and it does not exceed 45 or 50 metres (49·5–55 yds.). It would be sufficient to sink in the Canal a medium-sized warship, or even a big merchant vessel, to bar the road to trade traffic, to military transports, and to other men-of-war. The raising of a sunk ship is always a hard job; even in peace time it would take a good twelve days to lift up a big boat; the work is very complicated, you need a lot of dredges, barges, working men and so on. All this is absolutely impracticable when your enemy holds the approaches and is able not only to handicap the work, but even to sink your dredges at the side of the first victim. . . . I heard from people who know the Canal as their own pocket that a clever and well-equipped enemy could employ in some places a simpler and more effective method by blowing up a part of the eastern bank, in order to upset enormous masses of sand and stone into the water.

" Of course the Turk is not likely to have at his disposal all the necessary means to damage the Canal. But if some day in the future Palestine should serve as a base for a real great Power, equipped with all the devilries of modern technique —then, believe me, it would be quite another story.

" I asked your officers why they chose the Canal as their first line of defence instead of establishing this line just on the frontier of Egypt, between El-Arish and Akaba. The answer was : because of the desert. If the defenders of Egypt had met the enemy at El-Arish, they would have the desert at their back. They would suffer all the difficulties which now paralyse the action of the Turks : the remoteness from the base, the slowness of transport service, the lack of water, in one word—the desert. Because the desert does perhaps protect you a little if it is before you, but it kills you if it backs your positions. The least recoil, sometimes inevitable even in successful campaigns, throws you then just in the middle of sands where you get not one tiny hamlet to give you a backing, while your enemy has immediately behind him a whole country full of men and supplies.

" The only logical conclusion of all that is this : the military value of the desert is rather negative in your case. The proper defence of the Suez Canal cannot be secured unless you put between this precious strip of water and any future enemy a strip of land, combining two essential qualities : (1) It must be decently spacious, so as to permit large-scale operations; and (2) it must be inhabited and cultivable, fit to supply necessaries to an army of which it forms the background. This is an exact description of Syria, or at least of Palestine. I think it was Nelson who said of Tangiers : ' This port must belong to England or to nobody.' Palestine is to the Suez Canal exactly what Tangiers is to Gibraltar."

We think this long quotation from an unpublished source will not seem superfluous. Of course "it has always been British policy to avoid having land frontiers coterminous with those of great military States." When practicable, this is the wisest policy. The sea is an ideal frontier, because it allows no encroachments. But since the boundary between Egypt and

SYRIA AND PALESTINE

Syria *is* a "land frontier," we cannot see any advantage in its being a desert. Of all possible frontiers a desert is the one which makes encroachments easy, and more than easy: it is a constant invitation to infringe. It may be neighbour's land in theory, but it looks too much like no man's land and seems to repeat by its magnetic silence the old dictum which expresses the psychology of all the colonial wars in history: *res nullius cedit primo occupanti.* Let us remember here what has been said before of "the irresistible push towards culture-less spaces," and of the force of culture which secures frontiers better than any wall of bayonets.

Syria must become unquestionably French. Palestine can only fall within the British sphere of influence. Luckily, the line of demarcation between the two zones has been distinctly drawn, at the same time and in the same sense, by Nature as well as by History. Both point at the Lebanon. Geographically, it is the highest elevation of the Syrian plateau, and it cuts the coast in two like a sort of hedge. Historically, it has been autonomous and nearly independent since 1856; its inhabitants — Druses and Maronites — are distinct by race and creed from their neighbours of both North and South, and have developed distinct and higher standards of economic and social life. Accustomed as they are to independence, they might enjoy it still further under a treaty of neutralization, keeping at the same time the land-mark between French and British dominions.

XIII—THE ARABS

XIII

THE ARABS

THE Arab aspirations of national revival and independence cannot be formulated in a precise scheme. They are as vague as the conception of an Arab nation, the conception which forms their base. For little Macchiavellis of the kind of Nedjib Azouri, the author of "Le réveil de la nation arabe," the "Arab nation" means only—for the present at least—the Arabs of the Ottoman Empire. He does England and France the courtesy of leaving Egypt and Tunis out. But it is clear that genuine Arab Nationalists do not stop at frontiers established by foreigners, and for them the Arab nation embraces all the peoples speaking Arabic dialects from Morocco to Bagdad. All these enthusiasts—those of Pan-Arabia as well as those of half-Pan Arabia—forget that mere resemblance of languages does not form a united nation. The mark and the tie of a nation "one and indivisible" is consciousness of national unity. This essential condition is far from being fulfilled by the different tribes which inhabit the northern coast of Africa and Western Asia. No observer would have the courage to affirm that people in Morocco and Tunis, in Tripolitania and the Yemen, Syria and the Irak, feel as members of the same nation. So far those populations are divided by deep distinctions of history and custom; left alone through some unex-

pected withdrawal of their European protectors and Turkish rulers, they would
naturally form at least four or five States,
and even wars between them would not
be surprising. Of course the existence of
all these tribes, especially the fact that
they inhabit an uninterrupted strip of land
stretching from the Persian Gulf to the
Atlantic, might form one day the base for
an active propaganda of national unity.
This day, however, is still hidden in the mists
of the remotest future ; before it dawns
some of the members of the projected Pan-
Arabic nation will yet need to learn many
things which form the line between savagery
and the beginning of civilization. And to
learn them they will need European teachers
equipped with the necessary authority.

Certainly the different Arab agglomerations present different degrees of cultural development—or, perhaps, of cultural back-wardness. A curious thing about them is this : whilst in Europe intensity of civiliza-tion augments gradually from east to west, in the Arabic world it is exactly the other way. If we take the word " oriental " in its old traditional sense, *i.e.*, as the opposite of modern western ideas and customs, then real " oriental " life can be found only in the extreme west : in Morocco. The further eastwards from Tangiers, the more western it looks. Tunis is even more " European " than Algiers, and Cairo still more than Tunis. We speak of the aspect of capitals, but the same applies to the peoples. Morocco can un-questionably boast an idyllic percentage of illiteracy : almost 100%. Algeria, which is much more enlightened, possessed in 1913, for a Moslem population of 4,500,000, no more than 226 Mussulman primary schools, while about 35,000 Moslem pupils attended French establishments. Tunis, with 1,730,000 Arabs, has 1,320 Mussulman primary schools. The corresponding figure for Egypt is somewhat lower in proportion to population—3,799 "muktabs" in 1914; but 100,000 Egyptian Moslems attend various European schools, while in Tunis about 5,000 only follow their example.

The same scale can be applied to the religious and social conditions of these countries. Morocco is the land of Moslem orthodoxy, old-fashioned and undiluted; the conservative influence of religious brotherhoods, which are omnipotent in the Maghzen's dominions, permeates everything in family life, social relations, education, and statecraft. The further eastwards, the weaker become the brotherhoods, the more pronounced the signs of beginning modernization.

Algiers possesses already a small set of what might be called Arab intelligentsia; but they are opposed on one side by the so-called " Old Turbans," mostly rich landowners whose essential feature is dislike of ideas, projects and all similar trouble; on the other hand, the " Young Algerians " are estranged from the masses of the people by their modern education and religious liberalism; they present only an isolated handful of individuals without any actual weight in the life.

Tunis is quite different. It has a well-developed bourgeoisie, rich, organized, fairly educated for oriental standards, sensible and conscious of its own dignity. Here, too, the " Young Tunisians," as a party, are not very numerous, but they have a *milieu* around them more or less prepared for modern ideas. The two academies of the Regency—the ancient " Olive Mosque " and the modern Khaldounia—have a strong modernizing influence on thousands of students. The vernacular press of Tunis is well edited and well written ; but of course for leading Nationalist inspirations the Young Tunisians look to Egypt.

Egypt, whose conditions are too well known in this country to need special reference in this book, represents a further step onwards in the scale.

The national aspirations along the

Southern Mediterranean coast follow the same rule. Nationalism is a modern idea, primitive peoples are not able to conceive it ; their life is so full of genuine national substance that they need no special programmes or parties to reaffirm their nationhood. The stronger the encroachments of foreign spirit, the better the chances for a national movement. Thus Egypt possesses a Nationalist party whose influence cannot be overlooked ; its programme presents the essential features of the European racial aspirations, containing demands for autonomy and for recognition of Arabic as the only vehicle of all education. The platform of the Young Tunisians is far less explicit, especially in dealing with the question of language : it seems that the Tunisian Nationalists are rather in favour

of bi-lingual education. The programme
of the Young Algerians as expounded by
a deputation which visited some parlia-
mentarians in Paris in 1912, is rather a simple
plea for equal rights for natives and better
education than a display of real nationalism. Morocco, in its patriarchal back-
wardness, is not the soil where such
plants as programmes or parties can thrive.

Of course this scale of ours is only
approximately exact. The gradual growth
of modern spirit from west to east is
interrupted by Tripolitania, a country
wilder even than Morocco ; and the extreme east of the Arab world—the ▉▉▉▉
Yemen and Mesopotamia—represents a still
lower stage of civilization. Not so Syria.
Its condition is peculiar : on one side,
Turkish rule paralyzed its progress, leaving

the country far behind Egypt, Tunisia, and Algeria in every way ; and still, on the other hand, the town population of Syria can be regarded as the foremost element of the whole Arab race. This may be partially attributed to the competition of European Powers which invaded that country with hordes of religious and secular missionaries. It may also be explained by the presence of a considerable percentage of Christians among the native people. But it seems that the main cause of the superiority of the Syrian type is a question of race, of the powerful admixture of European blood which so many energetic and conquering nations left on this coveted coast. However it be, the national movement in Syria is the vanguard of Arabism, and many among the leaders of

Egyptian Nationalists are men of Syrian extraction.

We dwelt on these features of the Arab world in and outside Turkey not only because of the interest they may present in themselves. They must be kept in mind when we discuss Arab claims in connection with Turkey's partition. They clearly show that it is more than premature to speak of Arabs as of one nation stretching from Tangiers to Bagdad; even the Arabs of the Turkish Empire do not form a united nation, as Syria, the Hedjaz, the Yemen and Mesopotamia present radical differences which exclude any possibility of common self-assertion. At the same time it cannot be denied that the Arab world shows some essential conditions which might one day develop into national unity.

This eventuality ought not to be over-looked. Whether the formation of a united Arab Empire in the remote future would be a gain for the world's civilization is a question which we are not prepared to discuss. But for Europe it would certainly mean one of the greatest colonial disasters ever known in history. France would lose Morocco, Algeria, and Tunisia ; Italy would lose Tripolitania ; England would lose Egypt ; and we do not think the losses would stop there.

Many hundreds of pages could be written to show that the European rule has accomplished a great civilizing mission in those countries, and that its liquidation would prove a curse, not a blessing, to the Arabs themselves. We prefer, however, to leave this delicate matter untouched and to say simply that the Great Powers do not want to be turned out of the northern coasts of Africa, and, if they succeed now in establishing their rule on some parts of Asia Minor, they will not want to be turned out from there either.

This unshakable resolve to keep the whole Mediterranean Sea in European hands forms the firm ground on which any Arab claim must be discussed lest the discussion be useless and fruitless. The victorious Western Powers in dealing with Arab aspirations will certainly be governed by principles of justice and freedom, but they will also conform to the general interests of civilization and order; and above all they will obey the imperative dictates of their own self-preservation. They cannot be expected to suffer the formation of any community which would be likely to try, even in the remotest future, the part of an Arab Piedmont.

"Piedmont" is a political term which hardly needs explanation. We have only to add that the sympathy one generally pays to the rôle of Piedmont in the Italian Risorgimento does not necessarily imply that the world ought to hail the idea of an Arab Piedmont with the same enthusiasm. The Italian revival held beautiful promises which we miss, so far, in the case of Pan-Arabia. Nor would there be any probability of such a "Piedmont" succeeding in its endeavours to lead and rally the Arabic-speaking tribes. It would only—and certainly—succeed in forming a permanent nest of agitation, intrigue and trouble, and would hinder Europe in her peaceful leadership of the different Arab countries towards progress.

These considerations force us to think that the Arab claims can only have some chance of success at this moment if they are formulated with the utmost moderation. The independence of Syria, for instance, is clearly and hopelessly out of the question. Such a project would not only clash against the ancient and well-founded claims of France, but it would also be understood by France, Italy and Britain alike as a most fateful attempt against the security of their colonial empires. The geographical position of Syria at the gates of Egypt, and especially that peculiar character of its population to which we have alluded above, seem to suggest the rôle of Piedmont with a tempting emphasis which the Western Powers will be very careful not to encourage. It does not exclude the possibility, even the probability of some concessions calculated to flatter the Arab feeling—as for instance the appointment of an Arab Chief with hereditary dignity ; but the principality formed in this way would still have to be governed as a Protectorate.

Quite different is the position of the Hedjaz and the Yemen. The Hedjaz, the country of the Holy Cities, Mecca and Medina, is destined to play a leading part in the future development of Islam as a religion ; but the national idea, being a product of modern western thought, has so far no ground for growth in this primitive region ; nor does it seem likely that higher secular education, which forms the condition and the basis of real nationalism, could make quick progresses within sight of the Kaaba. Geographically, the Hedjaz is isolated by deserts and sea and has no immediate contact either with Egypt or Syria. Its independence would be politically harmless. At the same time it would be a happy concession to the Moslem world which naturally shrinks from any idea of Europeans interfering with the Holy Places of Islam. Indeed, as far as we can gather from many authoritative statements published up to date, all the Allied Powers are agreed on the principle of absolute independence of the Hedjaz. We can only add that, the question of the Holy Places apart, the same reasons speak for the independence of the Yemen.

XIV—THE GERMAN CLAIM

XIV

THE GERMAN CLAIM

IN the emergency of Turkey's partition
Germany will find herself in a peculiar
position. Of all the Powers which ever
coveted Ottoman heritage, Germany had
the widest ambitions. English, French,
Russian claims were always limited to
certain portions of Turkish territory. But
it is almost impossible to find a corner
of Turkey that has not been mentioned
in some Pan-German pronouncement as
belonging to the future lot of " Deutschlands Erbe." Armenia and Mesopotamia,
Syria and Palestine were treated, and

sometimes by quite responsible writers, as the natural ground for Teutonic expansion and colonisation. This all-embracing appetite gives Germany some right to affirm that she was never in favour of the dismemberment of the Ottoman Empire. Of course she preferred the annexation of a united and indivisible Turkey. And we must agree that this plan has virtually been carried out by the present alliance between the Central Empires and the Young Turks.

It is highly questionable, however, to what extent Germany would be able to earn the fruits of this policy, even if she and her allies won the war. The German crowd seems to take it for granted that a common victory would attach Turkey for ever to her Teutonic masters. But it is hardly possible that this sanguine opinion be shared also by responsible men in Germany who know too well what Turkey is. Only one of three things can happen to Turkey : the first is partition ; the second —such a complete victory which would leave the Ottoman Empire strengthened and able to exclude any foreign influence ; the third—the *status quo ante, i.e.,* the old Turkish system of fictitiously accepting the tutelage of all the leading Powers, in order to counterbalance one with another and to deceive them all. One thing only can never happen : Turkey will never suffer the exclusive predominance of *one* foreign Power. Those who dream of it show their ignorance of the A B C of Turkish history as well as of the mentality of the Young Turkish leaders. It is enough to have the slightest acquaintance of men like Enver, Talaat, Hamil, Djavid, Hussein-Djahid, to throw away any illusion of this kind. Of course Turkey will be very glad to accept Germany's military services—for instance, to admit again German instructors in her army and to allow the establishment of Krupp's factories in Turkish cities. But this kind of help, given by one State to another, produces one peculiar consequence : it obliges the State which gives far more than the one which receives. The country which is in need of these kind of services is never forced to beg for them, to entreat, to promise compensations in return. On the contrary, that country would be over-whelmed with offers and would only have the pleasant embarrassment of choice. And the happy winner would be very careful not to forfeit his privilege, and would be compelled to make all sorts of concessions to his " pupil," lest the latter should get tired and replace him by one of his competitors. This will be exactly the attitude Turkey will assume towards Germany if the war ends with a victory of the Central Empires. Fearing lest German influence might develop into an unofficial protectorate, the Young Turks, jealous of their independence, will have recourse to the old method: they will immediately try to make up with the Entente. No need to explain why their endeavours on this side will meet with the most cordial reception. So long as Turkey lives in the form of a great Empire any sort of one-sided foreign hegemony is out of the question. We are afraid that very soon after the " victory, " all the illusions of the German crowd would be bitterly deceived.

Turkey's partition will put Germany in a very delicate entanglement. For one thing, the hope to swallow the Ottoman Empire in one gulp will be gone, and will be replaced by the legitimate desire to secure at least some part of the heritage. On the other side, being an ally of Turkey, Germany cannot, for the sake of decency, take any positive part in Turkey's dismemberment. The humour of the situation may suggest to some people an easy and obvious reply—" then leave Germany out, and that's the end of it." We do not share this easy and obvious view. We think Germany cannot be left out; and if she were, it would not be the end of it.

THE GERMAN CLAIM

Fortunately this book appears at a time when people have dropped the foolish talk of " crushing Germany." Even defeated, Germany will remain a big Power—a Power in every sense, in wealth, culture, and military force. It will remain, above all, an admirable centre of energy. Energy needs expansion ; if prevented from expanding within reasonable limits it must cause an explosion. The policy of excluding Germany from any natural expansion would be, for us, a policy of suicide.

This does not mean that we consider the Entente's inner markets as a natural field for German penetration. If it will be found advisable to reserve these markets for the Allies' trade only, we do not think such protection could prejudice the durability of peace. But the outer, the " colonisable " world must not be closed altogether for either Germany or Austria.

Of this world, the Middle East is one of the most essential parts. The Drang nach Osten was an exaggeration in the colossal range of its claims, but in its essence it was a necessity. The Allied Powers will be well advised if they oppose the exaggerations but reckon with the indestructible needs of an indestructible organism.

The partition of Turkey does not mean the destruction of the natural home of the Turkish race. This home is Anatolia, the vast region which occupies roughly the protuberance of Asia Minor from the Ægean coast to a line corresponding to longitude 37. The country thus described includes the bulk of the Turkish nation, about 6 millions. With the exception of some coast districts where they are mixed with Greeks and Armenians, Turks are the only inhabitants of Anatolia. It is what we call a purely national territory, and this character will become still more pronounced if the district of Smyrna with 150,000 Greeks should be annexed to Greece and the region of Adalia should come under Italian protectorate. Being the cradle and the stronghold of the Osmanlis, Anatolia is also the best natural field for their development. Confined within the ethnical boundaries of their race, free from the burden of misruling 15 millions of other peoples who hate them, the Turks in Anatolia will be able at last to progress in the ways of order, culture, and wealth.

To accomplish this progress they will need European advisers and furnishers.

TURKEY AND THE WAR

If this task of leading the new and smaller Turkey towards civilisation could be left exclusively to Germany and Austria, such an arrangement would have two big advantages : it would correspond to that mutual inclination which expressed itself in the present Germano-Turkish alliance, and it would, at the same time, settle, in the fairest way, Germany's longing for a place in the sun in the Near East.

Of course the Turkish race in Anatolia is entitled to complete political independence. But Germany cannot pretend to establish any form of political domination over her own ally whom she promised to help in removing the last traces of western ascendancy in the Orient. Even offered by the victorious Allies a portion of the Ottoman heritage, Germany would be morally compelled to refuse it. This situation suggests a settlement equally fair to Germany and Turkey. Anatolia must remain an independent Sultanate—independent not only on paper, but in fact, just as Switzerland, Holland or Britain herself. At the same time, the Allies could sign a treaty with Germany renouncing, for a certain period of time, any claim on their part for the treatment of the most favoured nation in Anatolia. It would leave Germany free to conclude whatever commercial treaty she likes with the new Turkey— even to include her in the Zollverein. Without impairing Turkish sovereignty it would secure for Germany very considerable privileges in furnishing practically all the requirements of life and progress to a fairly populated country, about the size of Spain, prolific and capable of colonization, and in helping to exploit its great agricultural and mineral resources.

ꞏ To renounce this important field of commercial competition would be of course a not inconsiderable sacrifice for the Allies. But, we repeat, Germany must be granted a door for expansion in the East lest her vitality should compel her to knock one day with the mailed fist at our own doors.

APPENDIX—SOME MILITARY ASPECTS

XV—THE MAIN FRONT

XV

THE MAIN FRONT

WE hear only too often that laymen should not interfere with problems of strategy. It is doubtful whether this principle can be accepted unreservedly. Strategy (of course we do not mean tactics) has undergone the same change as diplomacy. Both used to be considered, in days gone by, as a sort of black magic, an occult science whose secrets were only open to highly trained druids. Nowadays the world has realized that any good man of business is able to make a good diplomatist. Perhaps one day the same will apply to strategy.

TURKEY AND THE WAR

" Military secrets " play only a part of secondary importance in modern warfare, and sound strategy is not based upon them. Sound strategy can be only based upon the realization of advantages or drawbacks of different theatres afforded by geography, economy, statistics of population, railway systems and so on—all matters of common knowledge. Naturally we do not suggest that laymen ought to lead strategical operations. But their right to criticize and to suggest is unquestionable, especially after so many mistakes have been committed by those who are supposed to be initiated in the druidical mysteries.

After this little preface, we venture to say that Turkey, and to be more exact Asiatic Turkey, is the main theatre of this war.

THE MAIN FRONT

The western offensive has already taught us the exact extent of its possibilities. We do not underrate its good effects, but the thing which matters—the " decisive blow " —is still out of sight, nor are there any signs of the probability of such an event in that corner of the world war. The progress of the Allies is wonderful, but it is slow, and its tempo can hardly be changed. We are told that it will gradually lead to the recapture of important French and Belgian towns, and so we believe. But in the same way as the capture of Verdun would not have meant the breakdown of France, the recapture of Lille, or even (let us be sanguine) the taking of Metz would not crush Germany. Of course it would be a tremendous blow to the Central Empires, it would mean a

radical change in the military situation;
but Germany's force of resistance would
still remain colossal and unimpaired. It
is better not to deceive ourselves. We
trust that the western offensive will con-
tinue with energy and success; but the
tempo of the advance and its immediate
effect on the co-relation of the belligerent
forces should not be exaggerated.

The same seems to apply to the Russian
front. Even there, we hope, Germany
will no more be given the opportunity of
administering dangerous strokes, and perhaps some day we shall yet witness a
revival of the Russian offensive; but the
steam-roller theory seems to be abandoned
in all quarters.

The only theatre where " decisive blows "
can be imagined is Asiatic Turkey. On

that theatre warfare seems to have kept its old character : smaller numbers of men and material, smaller losses as price of victory, and incomparably quicker territorial advance in the case of victory. This truth cannot be obscured by the two failures of Gallipoli and Kut : the causes of the melancholy results of the Dardanelles and Mesopotamian campaigns are sufficiently known, and these results do not prove anything except the danger of either negligent or half-hearted warfare. The Russian invasion in Armenia showed that, where neglect or half-heartedness are more or less avoided, enormous territorial successes might be won with forces which, on any European front, would prove insufficient for any serious push. Turkey cannot hold her own against Powers equipped with modern technique if they give the Asiatic front the whole effort it deserves. No German help can change this balance of forces. The German method of warfare, based on the greatest display of technique and organization, is only possible in countries where there is a thick network of railways, a dense and more or less civilized population, huge material resources. All these are wanting in Asiatic Turkey. German engineers may have considerably improved or developed the Bagdad and Hedjaz railroads, but this fact alone cannot have transformed Mesopotamia or the Sinai desert into anything like Champagne, Flanders, or even Lithuania —countries of trench warfare. Similarly, all talk pretending that Turkish troops, if stiffened by a little German starch, acquire at once all the formidable qualities of a real German army is mere gossip. Starch is not iron. With a quarter of the cost of a fortnight's offensive on any European front, the half of Anatolia, the whole of Mesopotamia and Syria could be invaded and occupied.

But this is not all. Turkey is not Germany in yet another sense. To break Germany's force of resistance would be a task of tremendous difficulty; we repeat that this result would not necessarily be achieved even in the case of the Allies eventually crossing the German frontier and carrying war into German territory. Behind the German army there are 65,000,000 of a highly cultured nation endowed with an enormous national pride, led by an old and haughty aristocracy, conscious of an almost inexhaustible riches in moral and material resources. To break the fighting strength of such a nation simply by physical blows is a long, very long business. But everybody who has the slightest knowledge of Turkey will agree that two or three serious strokes, like the capture of Erzerum, especially if occurring simultaneously on different fronts of her Asiatic dominions, would mean the collapse of her will for resistance. In other words, on the Middle Eastern theatre it is not only easier to advance, but the effects of advance are likely to have a much more decisive influence on the general march of affairs.

The consequences of Turkey's collapse are easily understood, and there is no need to repeat here what has been said many times. But one of these consequences ought to be emphasized again and again because its importance seems to be underrated by public opinion. We mean the influence which a Turkish *débâcle* would have on the German public's attitude towards the war.

Germany is largely a country of business men. Now the German business man does not bear the strain and the sacrifices of this war for the mere sake of national glory. He also delights in dreams of world power, but for him world power has a clear and simple meaning : larger markets. This is the prize for which he suffers, the hope which comforts him when the sacrifice begins to appear too heavy. Remove this object, and the war will lose, in his eyes, its justification.

TURKEY AND THE WAR

The hope cherished by the industrial and commercial classes of Germany is two-fold : it includes profitable commercial treaties with the Allies after the war—and an Ottoman Empire within the Zollverein. The first of these hopes has already received a heavy blow : we mean the Economic Conference in Paris which dealt with German trade in the Allied countries and resulted in proclaiming what may be termed " the annexation of German markets " within the Entente's own household. Many of us do not yet realize the full value of this blow ; others question its efficiency and declare, in the name of the holy lore called Political Economy, that prohibitive tariffs on such an enormous scale are " economically impossible." These sentences belong to the same sort of scientific prophecy we heard in such plenty at the beginning of the war, when we were told that it was " economically impossible " for the war to last more than a few weeks because in a few weeks all the world would be bankrupt. It is guess-work, not science. We feel sure that this easy-going appreciation of the Paris decisions cannot be shared in Germany. At the time of the Conference some German papers, of course, indulged in comfortable chatter about the " economic impossibility " of the Allies doing without German products after the war ; but the business men of Germany, with that instinct for realities which is their strength, feel and know that the doom of German trade is meant in earnest and càn be carried through without producing any irremedi-

able disturbance in the enormous household
of the Allies. Of course, the German
business man firmly believes in his nation's
ability to remove this menace at the end
of the war. Germany is, so far, well
equipped for the final bargain : she has
accumulated many precious pawns and,
so long as she holds them in her grip, the
Gross-Industrieller is confident that the
re-admission of his goods to their former
privileged position in the Allied markets
may yet be extorted at the Peace Conference in exchange for territorial evacuations.
But in this way the war, instead of being
a struggle for new acquisitions, is transformed in his own eyes into a war for
the re-establishment of the *status quo
ante*. Thus every business man in Germany is by now compelled to ask himself

and his neighbours: " Why this war, then ? "

The answer which he gets from his official comforters is obvious: " Turkey." There is one market which the Paris decisions cannot affect. It is one of the largest, one of the most various and most promising markets of the world ; it is at the same time an immense reservoir of raw materials. Turkey is the *ultima spes* of the German business man ; in the notorious scheme of a self-contented *Mitteleuropa,* which represents to German minds the only alternative to oversea expansion, Turkey is the vital link, the spring of the clockwork. If you strike at it the whole system collapses.

But the military occupation of this market cannot be achieved by conferences nor by legislation. It must be carried out by conquest—by establishing the Allies' garrisons in the various provinces of the Ottoman Empire.

So far, this task has not received all the attention it deserves. Of all the Entente's mistakes this 'one is the greatest. We forgot that Turkey is not only an ally whose collapse would weaken Germany's strength. Turkey is one of the principal aims of Germany's efforts, the *raison d'être* of most of her decisive acts and moves. The mob in the streets of Berlin may be dazzled by the idea of German troops camping in Belgium and Poland : leading and responsible men know only too well that Belgium must be restored and that Poland, whatever her fate may be, is not certain to remain under German control after the war. What encourages them is neither Belgium nor Poland—it is the connection of Berlin with Bagdad. The invasion of Turkey would mean not only the end of the weakest of Germany's allies : it would mean the end of the strongest of those reasons which make the war worth its cost in German eyes.

" I do not believe in psychological warfare," said a great general not long ago, " we must strike at the enemy's soldiers, not at his psychology." This sentence is often quoted, but it would sound much more convincing if it were less dogmatic. We must strike at both soldiers and psychology. Civilized nations fight for the sake of certain goals ; if these are removed the enemy's obstinacy cannot remain unshaken. Even in Germany the military

TURKEY AND THE WAR

caste can only retain its freedom of action so long as the bulk of public opinion comply with the necessity of " keeping on."

THE END

Printed in Great Britain by Wyman & Sons Ltd., London and Reading

WS - #0023 - 080524 - C0 - 229/152/15 - PB - 9780282947842 - Gloss Lamination